UNCTAD/ITE/EDS/1

UNITED NATIONS CONFERENCE ON TRADE AND DEVELOPMENT
Geneva

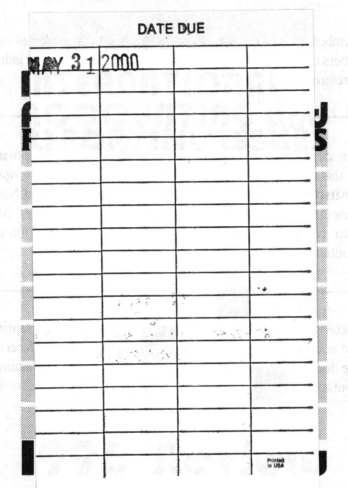

Environmental Accounting

**Report by the Secretariat of the
United Nations Conference on Trade and Development**

UNITED NATIONS
New York and Geneva, 1998

NOTE

Symbols of United Nations documents are composed of capital letters combined with figures. Mention of such a symbol indicates a reference to a United Nations document.

The designations employed and the presentation of the material in this publication do not imply the expression of any opinion whatsoever on the part of the Secretariat of the United Nations concerning the legal status of any country, territory, city or area, or of its authorities, or concerning the delimitation of its frontiers or boundaries.

UNCTAD/ITE/EDS/1

UNITED NATIONS PUBLICATION

Sales No. E.97.II.D.12

ISBN 92-1-112416-6

PREFACE

This volume contains the proceedings of the fourteenth session of the Intergovernmental Working Group of Experts on International Standards of Accounting and Reporting (ISAR), held from 1 to 5 July 1996 in Geneva. It was attended by government experts from over 50 countries and 6 NGOs. ISAR was created by ECOSOC in 1982 to promote the harmonization of national accounting standards. ECOSOC mandated it to work towards a global system for producing reliable and comparable financial information at the enterprise level. ISAR has done this over the past 14 years by promoting policy dialogue between developed and developing countries and by helping developing countries and countries in transition implement "best practices" whether in the form of directives of the Council of Europe or international accounting standards (IASs). This volume contributes to the spread of best practices since chapters I to VI contain the revised background papers and the major issues raised by the experts as well as their conclusions. The last chapter sets out the results of an ad hoc expert meeting which was intended to prepare the ground for the next meeting of ISAR.

The two most hotly debated topics on the agenda of the fourteenth session were compliance with IASs and accounting for commercial banks. The last three years (1994-1996) have been marked by a growing momentum in favour of the use of international accounting standards. Pressure has come from a number of sources. First, many TNCs find it burdensome to comply with different national reporting requirements when seeking listings on different stock exchanges. Second, the New York Stock Exchange would like to encourage foreign companies to use IASs when seeking a listing, so that it can maintain its market position *vis-a-vis* other bourses. Third, the International Organization of Securities Commissions (IOSCO) is encouraging the International Accounting Standards Committee (IASC) to produce a revised set of core standards which it can endorse for use by its member exchanges. Lastly, the European Union has indicated that it would prefer to increase its contribution to the work of the IASC and to keep the use of legislative instruments to a minimum.

However, we are still a long way from effective international accounting standards that allow TNCs to use one set of figures to raise capital in any market. This means that TNCs face a welter of conflicting regulations when seeking to raise capital. Both Daimler-Benz and Veba were forced by the United States Securities Exchange Commission to comply with United States Generally Accepted Accounting Principles (USGAAP) instead of IASs when seeking listings on the New York Stock Exchange in 1993. This resulted in confusion and embarrassment caused by the conflict between United States and German accounting rules. Under German rules, Daimler-Benz reported a profit in 1993 of over DM 600 million, but under United States rules a loss of over DM 1,800 million. These results were reversed the following year.

ISAR discussed the main reasons for national accounting differences, including unique historical events, external influences and the differing purposes of financial statements (i.e. for investment, credit and/or tax decisions). Some in the Group were dissatisfied with this traditional historical analysis of accounting diversity, and said it would have been more helpful to focus on the difficulties which developing countries have in adopting and implementing IASs. Representatives from developing countries confirmed that they had great difficulty in conforming with IASs, particularly when accounting rules were embedded in laws which were difficult to change. Thus, there is some merit in the traditional argument that codified law countries experience more difficulties than common law countries in complying with IASs. In addition, developing country representatives questioned whether IASs were applicable to small and medium-sized enterprises (SMEs). In concluding its discussion, the Group decided that accounting standards also needed to be harmonized for SMEs and that IASs should be reviewed to determine whether they meet the needs of all enterprises.

In taking up the topic of accounting for commercial banks, the Group was concerned by the fact that the banking industry has been marked by unprecedented growth, intense competition, rapid innovation and increasing complexity. Intense competition has resulted in banks' expansion into new and riskier areas of lending such as commercial real-estate and highly leveraged transactions or, increasingly, off balance sheet activities. At the same time, there has been a record number of bank failures in both developed and developing countries. Undoubtedly, disclosure practices have not kept pace with growth and innovation. The Group concluded that the recommendations presented in the banking paper adequately covered both the traditional and supplementary disclosures which banks should make so that users of their financial statements can assess their solvency, liquidity and profitability. Regarding risk management, the Group believed that banks should report on their internal control systems and their risk management performance.

The banking discussion was enlivened by the Forum on Bankers' Views on Disclosure by Commercial Banks. ISAR has always involved members of the accounting profession in its work. This is very much in line with the UNCTAD IX decision, in May 1996, to include civil society in the work of UNCTAD. The Forum brought the Group face to face with bank directors, managers, supervisors and auditors. It was chaired by Dr. Herbert Biener, Ministerial Counsellor, Ministry of Justice, Germany, who negotiated and implemented the European Council Directive on Bank Accounts. Forum participants insisted that accounting rules drive disclosure and that disclosure stimulates better risk management. The Group argued that the starting point for containing systemic risk for the global banking system had to be the accounting rules. Mr. Jurgen Krumnow, a member of the Board of Managing Directors at Deutsche Bank, explained why his bank was using IASs. "If you want to raise international capital, you have to play by international rules", he said.

The Group also discussed accounting for government concessions, transfer pricing, environmental accounting and work on the benchmark for professional qualifications. Environmental issues must be integrated into corporate accounting. Specifically, enterprise accounts should reflect a firm's environmental policies and the impact of environmental expenditures on reducing environmental risks and liabilities. In the long run these will influence the performance of the enterprise. There is a direct link between financial disclosure and eco-efficiency. The Group discovered in its first survey, in 1989, that there were no national accounting standards requiring environmental information disclosure. It formulated its first guidance on environmental disclosures in 1991, and this has stood the test of time. Leading experts believed that the ISAR proposals had to be the backbone for any company seeking to develop its environmental accounting. These were used to develop the recent proposals of the European Commission's Accounting Advisory Forum.

ISAR intends to develop more extensive guidelines for enterpises' reporting of environmental impacts in their financial statements. Such guidelines will assist government regulators and national standard-setters in drafting rules which meet the needs of users of financial statements. If issued in time, they will promote international consistency rather than diversity in the disclosure of environmental impacts.

For a number of years, ISAR has been concerned with the level of development of accountancy and accounting education worldwide. Developing countries, particularly in Africa, have a great shortage of qualified accountants, and this has considerable impact on accountability in these countries.

During the early 1990s, UNCTAD, the World Bank and the ILO surveyed the status of the accounting profession in Africa. The results were truly dismaying; half of the 35 countries surveyed had fewer than 50 qualified accountants each. The situation is the same in 1997. Almost every study of the quality of accounting and management information systems in developing countries has confirmed the correlation between the level of economic development and accounting development. If the financial management system is primitive, there can be no effective resource allocation or project management.

At its eleventh session, in 1993, ISAR considered developing a master plan for accounting education and certification. The objective would be to narrow progressively the education standards gap between the developed and developing nations to an acceptable level. There is a need to develop a benchmark that could be used by developing countries to assess the adequacy of their professional requirements. Work on such a benchmark would both strengthen the profession in developing countries and allow them to take advantage of reductions in the barriers to trade in accountancy services to be achieved by the WTO. This is consistent with the UNCTAD IX objective of extending technical assistance to developing countries to strengthen their service sectors, so as to help them reap the maximum possible benefits from liberalization of trade in services.

Currently, many different systems are being used to produce qualified accountants. A benchmark could evaluate these systems and reduce the time and cost invovled in assessing developing countries' credentials to see whether they meet developed country standards. Also, it would facilitate a common approach to educating accountants and auditors in developing countries so that different bilateral and multilateral projects produce consistent results and prepare accountants to enter a global profession.

In summary, the benchmark would establish a standard against which national accounting qualifications could be evaluated and would not act as a substitute for them. This would benefit developing and developed countries by:

- giving value to their national credentials;

- simplifying the process used during negotiations to recognize foreign qualifications;

- speeding up trade negotations and cutting costs, thus facilitating a cross-border trade in services;

- strengthening the accountancy profession, as national institutions provided better education to meet accreditation requirements;

- establishing international rules for a global profession.

At the fourteenth session, the experts discussed the future of ISAR. The restructuring of UNCTAD's intergovernmental machinery and the lapsing of ISAR's mandate provided an opportunity to discuss in what form the Group would continue its work. It has served as an intergovernmental body to review accounting and reporting developments, including the work of standard-setting bodies at the national and international level, since 1982. At the present time, ISAR is the only intergovernmental body which works as a catalyst for the harmonization of standards. It helps governments, especially those of developing countries and countries in transition, to understand new standards and at the same time express their views on these standards when they are still at the drafting stage. However, it is not enough to develop standards at the top. They must be applied at the national level. ISAR helps developing countries and countries in transition apply them through UNCTAD's technical cooperation projects.

The link between trade and investment flows and reliable financial information is obvious. Investors cannot make decisions in the absence of reliable, transparent and comparable financial statements. But, the fact that accounting is the nuts and bolts of our financial systems is often overlooked. Stock markets, banking systems or foreign direct investment flows cannot operate in the absence of accounting information audited by qualified auditors. Developing common accountancy standards and strengthening the accounting profession are fundamental for the proper functioning of financial institutions and investment flows, and thus for the cause of development.

Rubens Ricupero
Secretary-General of UNCTAD
Geneva, May 1997

Contents

Page

CHAPTER II
ACCOUNTING AND REPORTING BY COMMERCIAL BANKS

CHAPTER III

ACCOUNTING FOR GOVERNMENT CONCESSIONS AND OTHER BENEFITS

CHAPTER IV

COMPLIANCE WITH INTERNATIONAL ACCOUNTING STANDARDS

CHAPTER V

REDUCING BARRIERS TO TRADE IN ACCOUNTING SERVICES AND THE DEVELOPMENT OF A BENCHMARK FOR PROFESSIONAL QUALIFICATIONS

CHAPTER VI

REGULATION OF THE ACCOUNTANCY PROFESSION IN DEVELOPING COUNTRIES AND COUNTRIES IN TRANSITION

CHAPTER VII
CURRENT DEVELOPMENTS IN
ENVIRONMENTAL ACCOUNTING

Tables

CHAPTER I

REVIEW OF SIGNIFICANT CURRENT DEVELOPMENTS AT THE GLOBAL AND REGIONAL LEVELS IN THE FIELD OF ACCOUNTING AND REPORTING BY TRANSNATIONAL CORPORATIONS

SUMMARY

This chapter describes significant accounting developments at the national, regional and international levels. Included is information on pronouncements and work-in-progress of the International Accounting Standards Committee (IASC) and the International Federation of Accountants (IFAC), which represent the professional accountancy bodies. The activities of regional professional bodies are also reviewed. The chapter ends with a discussion of the main issues in accounting for financial instruments. Although IASC and some national standard-setting bodies have formulated standards for presentation and disclosure of financial instruments, including so-called derivative instruments, the more difficult and controversial topic of recognition and measurement of such transactions is still to be resolved. An important issue in this area is accounting for hedging transactions.

I. PROGRESS TOWARDS INTERNATIONAL ACCOUNTING STANDARDS

A. Introduction

The movement towards harmonization of accounting standards made significant progress in 1995. Since 1987 the International Accounting Standards Committee (IASC), located in London, and the International Organization of Securities Commissions IOSCO, located in Montreal, have been working together to secure wider acceptance of IASC's International Accounting Standards (IASs). Under the approach being proposed, companies wishing to issue securities in a foreign market would reconcile their domestic financial statements in accordance with IASs instead of the national requirements of the appropriate foreign capital market. By 1991 this approach was being followed in the United Kingdom and Hong Kong.

IOSCO has been encouraging IASC to improve its standards so that they become acceptable to all securities regulators. It was hoped that, if successful, this would result in a substantial increase in the number of foreign companies using IASs and listing their shares for trading on stock exchanges.

In October 1993 IOSCO formally endorsed the use of one of the IASs, IAS 7, Cash Flow Statements, and subsequently informed IASC that another 14 of the existing IASs did not require additional improvements. IOSCO's Technical Committee Working Party 1 on Multinational Disclosure and Accounting also formulated a listing of what it considered to be a set of core accounting standards to be applied by a company in preparing its financial statements for use in international securities offerings and other foreign capital markets listings.

At the July 1995 annual conference of IOSCO a press briefing was held on this matter and it was announced that the IASC Board of Directors and the Technical Committee of IOSCO had agreed on a work programme for the development of IASC's core standards. There is pressure to complete this programme by mid-1998, and resources are being increased to meet this accelerated deadline. The prospects for a successful conclusion of this exercise have been increased by a recent shift in attitude by the United States Securities and Exchange Commission (SEC) and the European Union. The SEC has said that it would permit the use of IASs by foreign companies wishing to list on United States stock exchanges, provided that current IASs are tightened. The European Union intends to increase its contribution to IASC's work and to keep the use of legislative instruments to a minimum. The Working Party on Professional Services of the World Trade Organization is also supporting the use of international standards as a method of facilitating trade in accountancy services.

B. Developments in the United States of America

One of the major impediments to the acceptance of international accounting standards was the reluctance of the United States, the largest capital market in the world. In July 1995 the United States Financial Accounting Standards Board (FASB) began work on a qualitative and comprehensive analysis of similarities and differences between IASs and the FASB's standards, for the purpose of understanding differences between generally accepted accounting principles in the United States and the current international accounting standards. It is hoped that some of the differences can be narrowed in the future.

In July 1995 the FASB held an organizational meeting with standard-setters in Canada, Chile and Mexico to explore areas in which the four countries could cooperate more fully in minimizing differences in their accounting standards. At this first meeting the standard-setters discussed their mission and plans for cooperation on financial reporting under the terms of the North American Free Trade Agreement (NAFTA). The agreed mission is to improve the overall quality and comparability of accounting standards among NAFTA members and to serve the information needs of users of financial reporting by enhancing their ability to analyse and compare enterprises.

With regard to IASC's work (see the section above), it is worth noting that the United States Securities and Exchange Commission has accepted use of IASC's IAS 7 (Cash Flow Statements), parts of IAS 22 (Business Combinations) and IAS 29 (Financial Reporting in Hyperinflationary Economies) by foreign registrants for the preparation of financial statements for securities offerings in the United States.

II. INTERNATIONAL ACCOUNTING STANDARDS COMMITTEE

A. New technical pronouncement

In June 1995 IASC issued International Accounting Standard 32, Financial Instruments: Disclosure and Presentation. The standard is effective for accounting periods beginning on or after 1 January 1996. It provides guidance on the classification of financial instruments amounts between their liability and equity components, including the presentation of related amounts of dividends, interest and gains and losses. Criteria are set forth for when assets and liability amounts should or should not be offset. The standard also provides guidance on the disclosure in the footnotes of interest rate risks, credit risks and the fair market values of financial instruments.

B. Work programme with the International Organization of Securities Commissions on a set of core accounting standards

This programme and the current status of its development are described in section I above.

C. Other projects in process

1. Financial instruments

The second phase of the financial instruments project (see section II.A above) began in February 1996 and deals with recognition and measurement issues, including securitization, debt defeasance and hedging transactions. A steering committee is preparing a discussion paper that examines the reasoning and assumptions underlying significant alternative approaches to resolving the major recognition and measurement issues associated with financial instruments, and the principles that should provide the framework for the development of specific standards.

2. Intangible assets

In May 1995 the Board of IASC approved Exposure Draft E50 on the above subject. It was circulated to interested parties and the comment period ended on 30 November 1995. The draft proposes requirements for the recognition of intangible assets, including internally-generated assets; measurement methods, including an allowed alternative of fair value amount when such valuation is determinable by reference to an active secondary market for the specific intangible assets; amortization; impairment of carrying values; and disclosures relating to intangible assets. The previous approach was based on the methodology for accounting for property, plant and equipment, but recognized that intangible assets have characteristics which require more restrictive treatments than do tangible assets. One of the more significant proposals was to limit the amortization period for intangible assets to a maximum of 20 years except where certain impairment tests are met and the reasons for believing that the useful life exceeds 20 years are fully disclosed. In the light of the comment letters received on E50, the IASC Board decided in March and June 1996 to revise the draft requirements for amortization of intangible assets and goodwill, and to propose instead that intangible assets and goodwill be amortized over their estimated useful lives, with no specified limit for the amortization period, but with a rebuttable presumption that useful life does not exceed 20 years.

In consequence, (a) the recoverable amount of intangible assets and goodwill should be calculated every year for those intangible assets and goodwill whose amortization period exceeds 20 years, and also every time an indicator of impairment is identified; (b) detailed guidance for indicators of impairment and requirements for the calculation of the recoverable amount of intangible assets and goodwill will be developed under the impairment project; and (c) additional disclosure will be required for intangible assets whose carrying amount exceeds 5 per cent of an enterprise's total assets. In addition, the IASC Board confirmed in March 1996 that accounting for development costs should be the same as for internally generated intangible assets. This will require no major changes in IAS 9 (Research and Development Costs). The Board considered in September 1996 three exposure drafts as a result of this project. These were IAS 9 (Research and Development Costs), IAS 22 (Business Combinations) and a revised Exposure Draft on intangible assets.

3. Presentation of financial statements

In June 1996 the Board approved the exposure draft on the presentation of financial statements. The proposed statement is intended to replace three existing IASs: IAS 1 (Disclosure of Accounting Policies), IAS 5 (Information to be Disclosed in Financial Statements) and IAS 13 (Presentation of Current Assets and Current Liabilities). The exposure draft covers:

(a)   the objectives and definition of financial statements;

(b)   concepts for presentation, including underlying assumptions; materiality and aggregation of information; offsetting of amounts and accounts; consistency of presentation; comparative information; and the selection and application of accounting policies;

(c)   the structure and content of the balance sheet and income statement, including objectives; minimum requirements for the face of each statement; and items to be presented either on the face of the statement or in the footnotes; and

(d)   the structure and contents of footnotes to the financial statements, including statements of compliance with international accounting standards.

An important new proposal is that financial statements should include a separate statement on non-owner movements in equity, listing certain items currently recognized directly in equity, exchange gains and losses, revaluations and their tax effects. IASC feels that the existence of this statement may assist in resolving some measurement issues in current and future projects, including the project on financial instruments.

4. Reporting financial information by segments

An exposure draft on this topic, E51, was issued in December 1995 and proposes amendment of IAS 14 on the same subject. It proposes changes in the way in which segments are identified for purposes of disclosing financial information about the products and services that companies provide and their operations in different geographical locations. The proposal also adds several new segment disclosures and eliminates others contained in IAS 14. Non-public companies would not be required to disclose financial information by segments. The comment period for this draft ended on 30 June 1996.

5. Earnings per share

In January 1996 the IASC Board approved Exposure Draft E52 on this subject. The draft proposes:

(a)   for companies whose shares are traded on public exchanges, that their published financial statements should report both basic and diluted earnings per share amounts on the face of the profit and loss accounts. Basic earnings per share is a defined term in the draft;

(b)   how earnings for an accounting period should be defined; and

(c)   the method of computing the number of shares outstanding.

The comment period on the exposure draft ended on 30 June 1996.

6. Income taxes

The Board approved a revised IAS on income taxes together with consequential changes to IAS 22 (Business Combinations).

7. Retirement benefits and other employee benefit costs

IAS 19 (Retirement Benefit Costs) was revised in 1993 as part of IASC's Comparability/ Improvements Project, and it became effective on 1 January 1995. A more comprehensive review of the subject matter of IAS 19 is now being undertaken to include post-employment benefits other than retirement benefits. Under discussion are the allowed actuarial valuation methods: the accrued benefit valuation method (considered as the "benchmark" procedure) and the projected benefit valuation method (as an acceptable alternative procedure). Also under discussion is the discount rate that should be used - whether it should be the expected return on a plan's assets or the interest rate on high-quality corporate bonds.

The steering committee for this project has proposed maintaining the approach whereby employee benefit obligations are recognized as a liability after deduction of any plan assets out of which the obligations are to be settled directly. Three methods for accounting for actuarial gains and losses are under consideration: deferred recognition; immediate recognition; and a "corridor" approach with immediate recognition in both the balance sheet and the income statement for items falling outside the corridor.

IASC has published an issues paper on this subject for guidance to the steering committee, for basic research purposes and for information for the Board members, who are considering the necessity for changes to existing guidance. The Board approved an Exposure Draft, E54, Employee Benefits, for publication in October 1996. Comments were due by 31 January 1997.

8. Accounting in agriculture

Agriculture is a significant activity in many countries, and the World Bank has provided funds to develop an accounting standard to improve the information provided to users of financial statements of agricultural enterprises. The IASC Board met in March 1996 and considered its steering committee's point outline for developing a methodology which will reflect the uniqueness of agriculture. First tentative conclusions have been reached.

In agriculture, biological growth and transformation may take place which may not be completely reflected in costs but which may contribute to asset and income growth. In some cases the costs associated with this growth and transformation are difficult to measure and they are therefore not allocated to the products produced. Also, it may be necessary to augment the usual accounting assumptions and add new concepts such as sustainability. The promulgation of an IAS on this subject is not expected until 1999.

9. Interim reporting

The Board approved in November 1995 a project on interim reporting for financial statements. It agreed that it is for national securities regulators and stock exchanges to decide which companies should be required to publish interim financial reports, how frequently and how soon after the period end. An interim report should include a condensed income statement, a condensed balance sheet, a condensed cash flow statement and limited disclosure notes. In general, costs should not be accrued or deferred as assets or liabilities at an interim date if they would not be similarly recognized at the end of the enterprise's financial year. Furthermore, the materiality of an item in an interim financial report should be assessed in relation to the period's figures, not estimated annual data. A draft statement of principles was issued in September 1996.

10. Discontinuing operations

In November 1995, the Board approved a project for developing accounting requirements for the recognition, measurement, presentation and disclosure of discontinued operations. It discussed a point outline in September 1996, and the steering committee published a draft statement of principles at the end of 1996.

11. Other

The Board approved project proposals (a) on provisions in March 1996 (the project will set out accounting requirements for the recognition, measurement, presentation and disclosure of provisions in the financial statements); and (b) on impairment of long-lived assets and on leasing in June 1996.

12. Interpretations of International Accounting Standards

In September 1996, IASC announced that in future it would issue interpretations of its IASs. The Board approved the formation of a Standing Committee on Interpretations (SIC). It will work closely with similar committees in individual countries and its interpretations will be subject to the Board's approval before they are issued. It will have eleven voting members from various countries and include individuals from the accountancy profession preparer groups and user groups.

III. INTERNATIONAL FEDERATION OF ACCOUNTANTS

The International Federation of Accountants (IFAC) is the worldwide organization for the accountancy profession. Its mission is to develop and enhance the profession to enable it to provide services of consistently high quality in the public interest. IFAC's programme of services for its members, which are national and regional professional accountancy bodies, is carried out by its governing Council and its seven standing committees: Auditing, Education, Ethics, Financial and Management Accounting, Public Sector, Information Technology, and Membership. It periodically forms ad hoc task forces for special purposes. IFAC, with headquarters in New York, has an extensive English-language publications programme and its members are encouraged to prepare and publish translations of its publications into local languages. Membership now stands at approximately 1,700,000 in 122 member bodies in 87 countries.

A. IFAC Council

In June 1995, the IFAC Council issued a Statement of Policy, "Implementation and Enforcement of Ethical Requirements". In addition to providing guidance on the enforcement of ethical requirements, the statement contains recommendations on how ethics discipline should be administered, the types of sanctions that should be imposed, investigation and appeal procedures, and what types of publicity should be given to disciplinary decisions.

Also at that time, the Council approved a Statement of Policy entitled "Recognition of Professional Accountancy Qualifications". The statement encourages member bodies to study the feasibility of recognizing the qualifications of accountants in other countries. Guidance is provided on the process to be followed, including which areas of education, experience and examination need to be scrutinized in pre-recognition investigations.

B. International Auditing Practices

IFAC's International Auditing Practices Committee (IAPC) issues International Standards of Auditing (ISAs) to lend credibility to the financial reporting process; to bridge the expectations gap experienced by users of audit reports by building public confidence in auditors' work; to contribute to consistency in national auditing practices; and to respond to current issues that affect auditors. ISAs when adopted by national bodies are intended to serve as easy-to-use guidelines for practitioners.

A major IAPC project was the codification and improvements initiative, concluded in June 1994. This project codified all the existing ISAs into one user-friendly format that is structured to follow the normal audit process, from planning to field procedures and finally to reporting and conclusions. The individual ISAs no longer are identified; rather, each issue is now dealt with in a "subject matter" section. The codification has provided an impetus for more and more countries to use ISAs as the basis on which national standards are set, and therefore to enhance harmonization.

In 1996 the IAPC issued an ISA on comparative financial statements and other figures that correspond with items included in a current period report. In 1995 it had issued a discussion paper entitled "The Audit Profession and the Environment". This document considers environmental matters in the audit of financial statements, environmental management systems and the auditing of their effectiveness, and audits of environmental performance and compliance. The comment period on the latter paper expired in September 1995 and guidance is expected to be issued in the future.

C. Education

International Education Guidelines (IEG) issued during the last two years are as follows:

(a)   IEG 9 (Exposure Draft), "Prequalification Education, Assessment of Professional Competence and Experience Requirements of Professional Accountants". This is a comprehensive revision of the existing IEG. It emphasizes the need for programmes to develop intellectual, interpersonal and communication skills and a commitment to high ethical standards and values.

(b)   IEG 11, "Information Technology in the Accounting Curriculum". This was issued to provide a framework for organizing an information technology oriented education programme and specifies the core areas of knowledge and skills that all professional accountants can be expected to possess. Pre- and post-qualification requirements are also described. In addition, the Education Committee has released a guidance paper on IEG 11 to assist educators in implementing the guidelines' recommendations. The report entitled "Integrating Information Technology across the Accounting Curriculum: The Experience of the Certified General Accountants Association of Canada" describes how that organization developed a programme of computer-integrated studies.

D. Ethics

In 1996 the IFAC Ethics Committee was replaced by an Ethics Forum and supporting Advisory Group. These two bodies have recommended several revisions to the current IFAC "Code of Ethics for Professional Accountants" in order to address new and changing issues. The revisions provide guidance on the use of long-standing senior audit personnel in audit engagements, professional fees, situations involving second and other opinions, and revisions to make the code more applicable to professional accountants in employed positions.

In March 1996 the Ethics Committee held its first Ethics Forum so that its member bodies could give the committee direct input for the development of new international ethical standards or additional guidance where indicated.

E. Financial and Management Accounting

The Financial and Management Accounting Committee has approved and released a revised statement on International Management Accounting Practices (IMAP) and two new statements during the last two years. These are as follows:

(a)   IMAP 3 (Revised), "Currency Exposure and Risk Management". The new statement emphasizes the role of the accountant in identifying and managing corporate currency exposure; describes the nature of specific forms of exposure; provides detailed formats for exposure reports; and refers to strategic means of managing foreign currency risk;

(b)   IMAP 6, "Post Completion Review". This statement provides guidance on assessing the efficiency and effectiveness of capital budgeting decisions by comparing planned actions with actual results obtained; and

(c)   IMAP 7, "Strategic Planning for Information Resources Management". This statement describes the principles and practices for information systems that can help to achieve an organization's objectives and enhance its performance. Five stages of the Information Resources Management (IRM) planning process are also described.

The Committee has also released three studies:

(a)   Study 3 (Revised), "An Introduction to Strategic Financial Management". This document provides updated guidance on the management accountant's role in managing change and contributing to an entity's long-term well-being. It sets forth the principles of strategic financial management and examples of applications.

(b)   Study 4, "Reporting Treasury Performance: A Framework for the Treasury Practitioner". The subjects covered include the objective of the treasury function in enterprises; the approach to risk management; the selection of performance measurements and definition of key controls; and the format of periodic reporting systems.

(c)   Study 5, "The Role of Management Accounting in the Emerging Team Approach to Work". This study was conducted to provide information on team-based work designs and processes, including self-directed work teams (SDWT), and how management accounting can contribute to the success of organizations with such teams.

A new series of booklets have been published recently by IFAC. These bring together the thoughts and writings of authors around the world on topics that are of current interest to persons in all phases of business enterprise. The booklets issued to date are:

(a)   "A View of Tomorrow: Management Accountancy in the Year 2004" (1994). This contains a series of articles with views on the future direction and requirements for management accountancy from the perspective of authors in several countries. The articles emphasize the speed of changes occurring in the world and the need for management accountants to have the appropriate knowledge in order to make a significant contribution to the success of their enterprises.

(b)   "A View of Tomorrow: The Senior Financial Officer in the Year 2005" (1995).   This booklet documents the views about the future of senior financial managers in companies throughout the world. Many of them feel that change must be managed in response to the globalization of business, developments in information technology and concerns about the environment.

(c)   "Performance Management in Small Business" (1996). This booklet deals with the steps required of the managers of small and medium-sized enterprises (SMEs) for achieving successful performance, and how management accountants assist managers in this process.

In 1994 the Committee began sponsoring an annual awards programme for articles on management accounting. Subjects vary, but all articles selected were published in various international journals and are being recognized as making a significant contribution to the advancement of management accountancy. In 1995 a publication was issued on outstanding articles written during the year.

F. Public sector

The Public Sector Committee has issued the following studies:

(a)   Study 3, "Auditing for Compliance With Authorities: A Public Sector Perspective";

(b)   Study 4, "Using the Work of Other Auditors: A Public Sector Perspective";

(c)   Study 5, "Definition and Recognition of Assets";

(d)   Study 6, "Accounting for and Reporting Liabilities";

(e)   Study 7, "Performance Reporting by Government Business Enterprises".

In addition, the following exposure drafts were issued:

(a)   "Definition and Recognition of Revenues" (the comment period ended in June 1996);

(b)   "Definition and Recognition of Expenses and Expenditures" (the comment period expired in May 1996);

(c)   "Proposed Study of Different Approaches to the Definition of the Government Financial Reporting Entity and Various Techniques for the Preparation of Appropriate Financial Reports" (the comment period expired in January 1995).

G. Other activities

During 1995 IFAC approved the formation of two new technical activities - the Membership Committee and the Information Technology (IT) Committee. The Membership Committee will deal with all membership issues, including membership criteria, admission procedures and relationships between IFAC and its members. In the initial phase it will also concentrate on helping the profession in developing countries to qualify eventually for IFAC membership. The IT Committee has a mandate to assist the profession in addressing the challenges that IT poses for the profession by issuing guidance and by making the member bodies aware of developments taking place throughout the world. Both committees have just formulated their respective work programmes for the next few years; they have yet to produce any guidance, although their work has begun.

In October 1995 IFAC made a presentation to the World Trade Organization (WTO), the successor to the General Agreement on Tariffs and Trade (GATT), on the regulation of professional accountants in its member countries.

IFAC sponsors a Capital Markets Forum as a vehicle for the discussion of a wide range of capital market issues, and participates in a group called the International Capital Markets Group (ICMG). The most recent ICMG publication is entitled "International Corporate Governance - Who Holds the Reins?" This report is a study of supervision process systems and practices in six of the world's major industrialized countries. ICMG has also released two discussion papers, entitled "Over-the-Counter Equity Derivatives" and "The Regulation of Electronic Securities Markets - Generally Accepted Principles and Regulatory Actions and Policies".

IFAC is now on the World Wide Web at http://www.ifc.org.

IV. EUROPEAN UNION

In 1995 the most relevant development in accounting in the region was the launching of a "New Accounting Strategy" by the European Commission (EC). The main objective was to fill the gap between the present financial reporting requirements in the European Union (EU) and the needs of international capital markets. This move was mainly determined by the fact that large European companies seeking capital on international markets are often requested to prepare a second set of consolidated accounts. This process is burdensome and costly, and besides constituting a clear competitive disadvantage for such companies, may generate confusion among users.

The new approach proposed by the European Commission will consist in enhanced collaboration between the Commission, the Member States and the various bodies dealing with accounting standards in Europe. The aim will be to keep the use of legislative instruments to a minimum and focus on consolidated accounts of large and listed companies. The common interpretations arrived at as a result of closer coordination are expected to result in both an improvement in the comparability of financial information reported in Europe and a much more effective European input into IASC's work.

For several years the Commission has been supporting the IASC-IOSCO initiative to agree on a core set of international standards to be used for multinational securities offerings (see above). Accordingly, one of the most important applications of the new accounting strategy will be to ensure that international standards remain as far as possible in line with the EC Directives. In order to make this possible, the EU Member States and the Commission undertook an in-depth comparison of the IASs with the EC Directives on accounting. It concluded that there are no material differences in practice between the directives and IASs. This should help European companies which want to use IASs without conflicting with European legislation.

Important progress has also been made in the field of accounting for environmental issues. The Accounting Advisory Forum (a European Commission advisory body composed of representatives from standard-setting bodies, the accounting profession, and organizations of users and preparers) finalized in November 1995 its document entitled "Environmental Issues in Financial Reporting". This report contains a set of guidelines on how to reflect environmental considerations in company individual and consolidated accounts and constitutes an important step forward in ensuring that the impact of environmental risks and liabilities on a company's financial position is fully disclosed to the public.

V. CONFEDERATION OF ASIAN AND PACIFIC ACCOUNTANTS

The Confederation of Asian and Pacific Accountants (CAPA) has 700,000 members in 31 national accounting organizations in 22 countries within its region (including two national organizations of accounting technicians). Its mission is to develop and enhance the accounting profession in the Asian-Pacific region to enable it to serve the public interest with services that are of a consistently high quality. CAPA holds regular conferences aimed at fostering closer ties between members and representatives of professional bodies in their region. Such conferences are organized at least three times in any ten-year period. The 14th CAPA Conference was held in Kuala Lumpur, Malaysia, from 7 to 9 October 1996.

Six times a each year the organization publishes a magazine - the *CAPA Chronicle* - and maintains a home page on the World Wide Web (http://www.jaring.my/webpres/capa). Some of CAPA's activities for 1995 and 1996 include:

(a)   Building stronger links with emerging and developing nations. A number of activities are being undertaken by CAPA and its constituent member organizations with a view to identifying and offering appropriate assistance to emerging and developing nations so that they can participate more effectively in world forums. This includes nurturing and encouraging the local accounting professions to adopt internationally accepted accounting standards which will enable the profession in those countries to play a major role as a catalyst for economic growth. By monitoring developing nations CAPA also hopes to be able to offer appropriate and timely assistance towards the development of local accountancy professional bodies in Afghanistan, Bhutan, Cambodia, the People's Republic of China, Laos, Maldives, Mauritius, Mongolia, Myanmar, Nepal, Solomon Islands, the Pacific islands and Viet Nam.

(b)   Assistance to Mongolia. Following a request from the Government, the Japanese Institute of Certified Public Accountants and the Korean Institute of Certified Public Accountants are assisting the Government of Mongolia in the transition to a market economy. The two organizations are promoting the development and training of accountants and auditors and the formation of a professional accountancy body.

(c)   CAPA Model Constitution and By-Laws. Through the efforts of the Australian Society of Certified Practising Accountants and the Hong Kong Society of Accountants, CAPA has developed a new Constitution and By-Laws for the Papua New Guinea Institute of Accountants. This project has resulted in the preparation of a draft model constitution and by-laws for use by other national accounting organizations. The draft is available in hard copy and computer diskette from the CAPA secretariat in Kuala Lumpur.

(d)   Development of competency guidelines for accounting technicians. This project by the New Zealand Society of Accountants aims to develop an overall framework for the appraisal of competency skills of accounting technicians. It is felt that the adoption of such a framework will be a positive first step towards facilitating cross-border recognition of professional qualifications.

(e)   Continuing Professional Education (CPE) for Professional and Technician Level Accountants. A guide to CPE is being compiled by the Cost and Works Accountants of India as a recommendation for accounting bodies.

In its programme for emerging nations, the CAPA secretariat has stated that it believes that there is much synergy to be obtained by collaborating with international organizations such as the Asian

Development Bank, UNCTAD and the World Bank on projects of mutual interest, and that it looks forward to exploring such possibilities with interested organizations.

VI. FEDERATION OF EUROPEAN ACCOUNTANTS

The Federation of European Accountants (FEE) is the representative organization for the accountancy profession in Europe and, in addition to providing direct services to its members, it advises the European Commission on accounting, auditing, taxation, company law and related areas. Its members comprise 34 professional bodies in 22 countries with a combined membership of approximately 350,000 persons. It has approximately 20 working parties active in a wide range of interests and activities for its members.

In early 1996 FEE launched a new programme of initiatives to address the needs of small and medium-sized enterprises (SMEs). Current projects in this area include:

(a)   development of a basic set of financial management tools and instruments for SME managers and auditors;

(b)   a research study on non-financial measures of performance used by SME managements. The report will be based on company case studies;

(c)   a research study on financial management instruments used by SMEs. The first sectoral report, based on the responses to a questionnaire, will be on the food industry;

(d)   a study of the costs of complying with tax laws for the various jurisdictions with authority over enterprises. Such compliance is disproportionately higher for SMEs than for large enterprises; and

(e)   an examination of the business operations that are within and outside the scope of value added taxes (VAT), and the formulation of criteria for the assessment of such taxes on financial services.

In the last few years, FEE and IFAC have been very active in monitoring and advising the World Trade Organization's Working Party on Professional Services, which is currently studying ways to reduce barriers to trade in accountancy services.

In 1994 FEE organized a workshop on the role of accountants in providing environmental audit services, and in 1995 it sponsored a seminar on "Environmental Stewardship and Management: Positioning the Accountancy Profession". The conclusion reached at the seminar was that the accountancy profession needs to play a more active role in both environmental accounting and auditing in the future. Accounting professionals need to be aware of developments in these fields; should be able to evaluate the consequences of environmental issues for enterprise accounting, and regularly schedule financial statement audits and management controls and information systems consultancies; should receive training in appropriate subjects; and should cooperate with other experts in the field and participate in multidisciplinary teams that work in areas related to environmental protection.

Recent publications, which may be ordered from FEE's headquarters in Brussels, Belgium, include the following:

(a)   "Report on the Role, Position and Liability of the Statutory Auditor in the European Union". In Europe the scope and coverage of the statutory audit varies from State to State. The report calls for moves within the region to clarify the laws under which statutory auditors report compliance; to clarify responsibilities for reporting illegal acts; and to assist statutory auditors when there is evidence that a client company may not be a "going concern". Other matters included in the report relate to the auditor's objectivity and his or her relationship with a client's management and shareholders.

(b)   "Survey of Pensions and Other Retirement Benefits in European Union and non-EU Countries". The survey addresses social, legal and institutional aspects of pensions and early retirement plans; accounting for pensions and early retirement costs; reporting and disclosure requirements of pension funds and insurance companies; and the role of actuaries and auditors in these schemes.

(c)   "Survey of Treaties Against Double Taxation". This is a survey of the incidence of double taxation laws and treaties against double taxation in EU and selected non-EU countries.

(d)   "Position Paper on Audit Independence and Objectivity". This paper addresses the primary means by which auditors can demonstrate that they can perform their duties in an objective manner, including issues such as relationships between the auditors and the enterprise being audited; the relationship of the fees for performing auditing services to the total revenues of the professional firm; and the appointment and rotation of auditors.

(e)   "Survey of the Activities of Professional Accountants in Europe". This survey is a detailed analysis of the role of European accountants and auditors in the business community.

(f)   "Environmental Accounting and Auditing: Survey of Current Activities and Developments within the Accounting Profession". This survey, issued in 1995, updates a previous survey and presents the current situation of environmental accounting and auditing in each of the European countries.

(g)   "Investigation of Emerging Accounting Areas". This 1994 study analyses trends in disclosures; environmental issues; goodwill; capitalized intangible costs; accounting for associated companies and joint ventures; and product liability matters.

(h)   "The Form and Content of the Consolidated Financial Statements of Financial Conglomerates". This report discusses matters such as the consolidation of banking with insurance operations; valuation rules; and technical problems that are encountered in combining different operating activities.

(i)   "Discussion Paper on Responsibilities for Financial Reporting by Companies". This paper considers the needs and expectations associated with corporate financial reporting and the relationships among all interested parties.

(j)   "Discussion Memorandum: Comparison of the Prudence and Matching Principles". This paper provides a comparison and analysis of the application of these two basic accounting concepts, in terms of both the laws and the accounting standards which govern the practices for specific transactions.

VII. CO-ORDINATING COUNCIL ON ACCOUNTING METHODOLOGY IN THE COMMONWEALTH OF INDEPENDENT STATES

The 5th session of the Council was held in Almaty, Kazakhstan, during September 1995. Its activities are funded by the OECD. An important topic discussed was the status of accountancy training in selected countries of the Commonwealth of Independent States (CIS).

A conclusion was that training has to be closely integrated with reform of the accounting and reporting systems for enterprises, in both the public and private sectors. However, before reform can take place a nation's policy makers need to be made aware of the issues, particularly the need for reform and the specific matters to be addressed. When new regulations have been finalized and promulgated, the accounting practitioners can then be trained in what has changed. To be successful, the persons responsible for the reforms need to be deeply involved in the retraining process.

To date, reform has occurred at a slow pace in the CIS countries despite numerous aid programmes. There are several obstacles to reform. First, there is little support for accounting reform at the policy-making level because ministers of finance have not grasped the fact that such reform is an essential part of financial reform. Second, tax officials fear that if accounting rules change tax revenues might decrease. With growing budget deficits and pressure from the IMF and the World Bank to increase tax collection, tax officials often block reform. Third, there is difficulty in distinguishing between laying down general accounting principles which are valid for all enterprises and financial institutions and writing detailed accounting standards. Some CIS accountants want to combine the principles which belong in a conceptual framework with detailed standards which are the practical guidelines for presenting accounting information. This makes a universal conceptual framework for the CIS hard to achieve since the developers disagree on the amount of detail needed. Fourth, standard-setting is being fragmented among various agencies such as the Ministry of Finance, the Commission on Securities, the Central Bank and the state insurance agency. These bodies do not see that the basic accounting principles should apply to all entities and that their efforts should be confined to formulating the special accounting requirements needed by entities under their jurisdiction. Lastly, the lack of comparability among Western accounting systems is also a problem. Experts, who come from either the Anglo-Saxon tradition or the Continental one, tend to promote their own national systems rather than EC directives or international accounting standards.

A. Russian Federation

For several years, the European Commission has financed the work of a consultative body known as the International Advisory Board on Accounting and Auditing Developments in the Russian Federation (IAB). It is composed of both national representatives and international organizations such as IASC, IFAC, OECD, UNCTAD and the World Bank. The EC has provided consultants for its work. Draft accounting and auditing laws have been formulated. The accounting law was passed by Parliament in 1996 and signed by the President after being vetoed twice. The auditing law has yet to go before Parliament.

The EU project also contains a training element. A team of national and international consultants have formulated a curriculum for 16 weeks of intensive training in accounting and auditing. This project is unique in that the material was developed in Russian by Russians for Russians and reflects the current legislation and the way in which it is likely to develop. Previous training courses used translated materials which did not reflect the Russian environment. Professionals from the seven largest international firms of independent accountants worked with leading Russian academics. Pilot courses were run in both Moscow and St. Petersburg for 50 trainers to test the materials. However, more must be done to ensure the quality of the profession. Audit certificates are currently being issued after a training period of a few weeks, whereas the norm in the West is three to five years, often after a relevant university degree has been obtained. There is a need in the Russian Federation and throughout the CIS to upgrade the syllabus in all teaching institutions and tighten the professional examinations before a comparable standard can be reached.

B. Uzbekistan

In Uzbekistan, UNDP and EU/TACIS funded UNCTAD and KPMG respectively to undertake an accounting reform project. The project revised the production cost regulation, which was subsequently implemented by the Ministry of Finance. The effect of this regulation was to delink financial accounting from tax accounting. The project also drafted new accounting and auditing laws. The accounting law was adopted by Parliament, and the auditing law is under consideration by Parliament. In addition, formats for new financial statements for enterprises and a revised chart of accounts were formulated. This was followed by an extensive training programme. Over 3,000 practitioners were trained in the new production cost regulation that were instituted by the Government as of 1 January 1995.

VIII. OTHER IMPORTANT INTERNATIONAL RESEARCH: JOINT REPORTS OF STANDARD-SETTING BODIES

In the interest of contributing to the harmonization of accounting standards, a group of standard-setting bodies jointly undertook research and issued reports on three topics in 1994 and 1995. The group comprised the Australian Accounting Standards Board, the Canadian Accounting Standards Board, the International Accounting Standards Committee, the United Kingdom Accounting Standards Board and the United States Financial Accounting Standards Board. The reports are intended as discussion papers for use by standard-setters in promulgating national and international accounting standards.

The first research report, issued in 1994, was "Future Events: A Conceptual Study of Their Significance for Recognition and Measurement". It addresses factors that should be considered when recognizing and valuing assets and liabilities in the current accounting period. When costs are incurred in one period this may or may not result in an actual or probable future benefit - that is, a reason for the recognition and recording of an asset. Also, a current obligation must actually or probably exist as a reason for the recording of a liability in the current accounting period. The measurement factors identified for consideration include the probability that expected future events and changes in legal requirements will occur, and the effect of current economic conditions on future measurements of assets and liabilities.

The other two reports were issued in 1995. The first of these was "Major Issues Related to Hedge Accounting". It describes risks and exposures to risks and how risk reduction is attempted. Hedging and accounting for hedging transactions is a complex area. Several examples of hedging transactions are discussed, along with alternative special accounting treatments, including the deferral of gains and losses. The report concludes with a description of the accounting issues for some financial instruments, such as options, that are commonly used for hedging risk exposures.

"Provisions: Their Recognition, Measurement, and Disclosure in Financial Statements" was the third report. It points out that provisions (which are the recording of liabilities in respect of which there is uncertainty about the accuracy of the amounts and the timing of possible transfers of economic benefits to others) are often material in reporting the financial performance of an enterprise. Several issues are involved: when a provision should be recognized; when it should be measured; and what should be disclosed about it. The report includes the application of the principles contained therein to provisions for future operating losses and for restructuring costs.

IX. ACCOUNTING FOR NEW FINANCIAL INSTRUMENTS

The most significant area of research currently being studied by international and national standard-setters is accounting for financial instruments, and particularly for derivative financial instruments (usually referred to simply as "derivatives"). ISAR first reviewed this matter at its twelfth session, in 1994. One of the reasons for attention being directed towards this area of financial reporting is that the volume and the value of transactions involving these instruments are increasing at exponential rates in most of the countries of the world. Managers of enterprises are increasing their use of derivatives in their efforts to manage risks that exist in their operating environment, including interest rate risks, foreign exchange risks and price risks.

Another reason for the significance of the research is the notoriety that has been given in the press to substantial losses incurred by financial and non-financial institutions and the perception by the business community that the current financial reporting standards may be inadequate. Users of financial reports are confused or, worse, are being misled. Clearly, there is an urgent need for transparent financial reporting of financial instruments because of their current economic importance in most countries.

Derivatives may be defined as those financial instruments whose values are based on other financial instruments or transactions. They have been purchased by enterprises for at least 20 years and include such common items as commodity options and forward currency contracts. Historically, they have been used for what is referred to as "hedging", that is to offset or reduce a perceived risk of an adverse consequence occurring. For example, one common type of hedge is against a negative change in the foreign exchange rate between two currencies: the currency of a domestic company and the currency of a company in a foreign country with which it has entered into a sales transaction require payment of an agreed amount denominated in the foreign currency. In this situation, the seller enterprise might want to hedge the risk that there would be an unfavourable change in the currency exchange rates between the two countries before the seller receives its payment.

In the global economic market-place the seller enterprise has an alternative, which is to hedge or protect against any risk of loss from exchange rate fluctuations by entering into a contract to sell on the date it expects to collect a certain amount in a foreign currency an equal amount of the foreign currency at the current exchange rate between the two currencies. In this way the seller enterprise is assured that the current exchange rate will be realized when it collects its account receivable and converts the foreign currency received to its domestic currency. Most of the non-financial transnational corporations feel that they are not in the business of taking these types of risks. Of course, the enterprise pays a fee when entering into such a transaction (called a foreign currency forward contract) to the bank or other organization or individual that agrees to purchase the foreign currency amount at a future date at the agreed exchange rate.

Another common type of derivative transactions is futures contracts. Such contracts may be entered into for the purchase or the sale of specified quantities of financial or non-financial items, commonly commodities. For example, an enterprise may know that it will need a certain quantity of a commodity at a certain date and wish to establish (fix) the price of that commodity at the current date. The enterprise can enter into an agreement to buy the specified quantity of the commodity at a future date at a price that is determinable at the current date. Obviously, for every purchaser of such a contract there must also be a seller who wishes to establish a certain price at the current date for a quantity of a commodity that it knows that it will wish to sell at a future date. There are, however, financial speculators in commodity futures contracts. Commodity option agreements such as these are very common and are entered into on national exchanges in many countries.

There are many other types of derivative financial transactions, too numerous to describe, such as options, swaps, collateralized mortgage obligations, floating rate notes, indexed securities, interest-only strips and principal-only strips.

Two accounting concepts apply in connection with financial transactions. The first is that transactions should be recognized, measured, recorded and reported in the accounting period in which they occur. The second is the matching principle - that is, the concept that revenues and costs and expenses that are directly related to each other should be recognized in the same accounting period. Without the appropriate accounting it is possible that a hedging financial instrument or the position being hedged might be recognized as a profit or loss in different accounting periods if one component terminates before the other. The difficulty in determining the most appropriate method to reflect the economic effect of often complex financial transactions is the cause of the debate among standard-setters, the financial community, enterprise owners and managers and others at the present time.

In order to adopt appropriate standards for accounting for financial instruments the following issues need to be addressed by standard-setters:

(a) When should a financial instrument be recognized, measured, recorded and reported in financial statements as an asset or a liability, and when should it be shown outside the balance sheet as an item for footnote or other disclosure?

(b) In general, when a financial instrument is to be reported in financial statements at a reporting date, how should it be valued, i.e. measured? Alternatives are:

(i) historical cost;

(ii) current (fair) value, i.e. mark-to-market;

(iii) the lower of historical cost or current value; or

(iv) some other basis.

(c) When realized and unrealized gains and losses are reported in statements of profits and losses, where should they be reported in relation to the net income amount?

(d) If financial instruments are recorded and reported at their historical amounts, how should such amounts be accrued or amortized over time?

(e) Some financial instruments that have been issued have component characteristics of both liabilities and equity. How should such instruments be reported by their issuers?

(f) There are some financial instruments which involve the transfer of certain rights and obligations, but the transferor might maintain involvement with the specific assets or liabilities. For such transactions, when should reporting of the assets or liabilities in the financial statements be discontinued?

(g) If a financial instrument has been purchased or sold as a hedge in order to manage an identified actual risk or a risk from an unrecognized purchase commitment or from anticipated future revenues, how should it be valued or measured at financial reporting dates? Alternatives are:

(i)   mark-to-market valuation;

(ii)   use of the deferral method of accounting; value the instrument at its historical asset or liability amount with any changes in the subsequent value deferred (that is, not recognized) until the date on which the change in value of the position being hedged is recognized as income or loss; then recognize the corresponding change in the value of the financial instrument at the same time; or

(iii)   report any changes in the current value of hedging financial assets or liabilities as one of the accounts in the equity section of the balance sheet until the date on which the change in value of the position being hedged is recognized as income or loss; then recognize the corresponding change in the value of the financial instrument at the same time in the statement of profit and loss.

(h)   If it is determined that the carrying value of a recorded financial asset has become impaired, when and how should the loss in value be reported in financial statements?

(i)   Assets and liabilities as well as firm commitments to acquire assets or incur liabilities might be hedged and be subjected to hedge accounting standards. Should the same rules be applied to hedges of cash flow exposures for future sales and purchases and interest receipts and payments that involve only expectations of future assets and liabilities as are applied to existing rights and obligations?

(j)   At the date on which a financial instrument is purchased or sold as a hedge, should the difference between the historical cost and the current value of the item or position being hedged be recognized as a gain or loss in the statement of profit and loss?

(k)   When should financial instruments be reported in the balance sheet as part of the related carrying amount of an asset or liability being hedged, and when should they be reported as separate assets or liabilities?

(l)   When should financial assets and liabilities be offset against each other?

X. WORLD CONGRESS OF ACCOUNTANTS

The next World Congress of Accountants will be held from 26 to 29 October 1997 in Paris, France. The theme will be "Accountants and Society: Serving the Public Interest". Those interested in attending should contact the organizers, S.O.C.F.I., 14, rue Mandar, 75002 Paris, France.

At the same time the International Association for Accounting Education and Research will hold its eighth world congress for accounting educators - "The Changing World of Accounting: Global and Regional Issues" (Paris, 23-25 October 1997). Contact IAAER, Congress, 153 rue de Courcelles, 75817 Paris Cedex 17, France.

CHAPTER II

ACCOUNTING AND REPORTING BY COMMERCIAL BANKS

SUMMARY AND CONCLUSIONS

The banking environment has changed dramatically in recent years. The financial industry has been marked by unprecedented growth, intense competition, rapid innovation and increasing complexity. This situation was the result of events such as the globalization of capital markets, the deregulation of financial activities, the involvement of non-financial institutions in the securities industry and the development of new financial instruments.

Intense competition has resulted in banks' expansion into new and riskier areas of lending, such as commercial real-estate and highly leveraged transactions or, increasingly, off balance sheet activities. Banks have expanded their role as dealers in derivative products.

At the same time, disclosure practices have not kept pace with this growth and innovation. Rapid change has outstripped the ability of current accounting and reporting regulations to accurately reflect the profitability and risks of commercial banks. Users of financial statements need to be able to assess the performance of banks from the perspective of investors and also from the perspective of depositors. This is even more important because of the unique role of financial institutions - that is, to provide risk-free safekeeping for property. Therefore, the users of financial statements of commercial banks need to be able to assess solvency, liquidity and profitability. To do this, they need information about a bank's risk exposure and risk management, investment portfolio and financial performance.

This chapter presents recommendations for broader disclosures by banks. In the interest of greater transparency and comparability, a universal disclosure system is promoted by providing guidance for standard-setters with responsibilities for commercial banks.

ISAR's discussion concentrated on four main issues:

- The need to improve risk management within commercial banks and the advisability of banks' reporting on their internal control systems and their risk management performance. It was suggested that ISAR consider developing guidelines for reporting on internal control systems and that these systems be expanded to deal with risk management and be headed by a "risk controller";

- Standard-setters need to give additional consideration to disclosure of related-party transactions, hidden reserves and limits on provisions for bad debts by tax authorities;

- Banks should clearly disclose the purpose of derivative transactions, whether it is trading, hedging or speculation; the common minimum framework suggested by the Basle Committee on Banking Supervision and IOSCO should be considered by banks;

- Many developing countries were concerned about adjustments for inflation since the capitalization of many banks was being eroded by hyperinflation; on the other hand, some developed countries felt that market values should be adjusted by "value at risk". Clearly, there was a need for guidance on the concept of "fair value".

The following specific remarks were made by the members of the Working Group.

Representatives of a number of African countries said that they were currently developing or reviewing laws and regulations on accounting and reporting by commercial banks and that the paper prepared by the secretariat on this topic was very important and useful. The representative of **Tunisia** said that there should be a separate statement that highlighted a bank's risks. He believed that it was necessary to assess these risks several times a year. The representative of **Morocco** said that his country was in the process of accounting reform in the banking sector and that the secretariat's report would be most useful. His country currently required two additional statements by banks: one on indicators of the quality of management and the other on sources of financing. The representative of **Gabon** said that the Central African Customs and Economic Union (UDEAC) was revising the accounting standards for banks and other establishments adopted in 1979. The secretariat study on accounting and reporting by commercial banks would thus be extremely useful to the Central African Banking Commission (COBAC) in finalizing the new accounting standards and bringing them into line with international accounting standards. The representative of **Nigeria** referred to the alarming rate of bank collapse due to fraud (30 banks in less than two years) and said that his Government had passed a Failed Banks Act. Embezzlement was a problem faced in all countries, and greater transparency and more comprehensive disclosure could assist the relevant authorities and other interested parties in detecting this illegal practice.

The representative of **Brazil** noted that deregulation of the banking sector was taking place in a period of rapid innovation in terms of the introduction of new financial instruments. This was a challenge for bankers, lawyers and accountants. There was a need for transparent accounting to report on these new instruments and to deal with adjustments for inflation. In particular, guidance on these topics was needed by developing countries. The representative of the **Democratic Republic of the Congo** concurred that adjustments were urgently needed to deal with inflation. The Group had considered the topic of hyperinflation and should continue to do so. In his country, banks had reached the verge of bankruptcy, as their capital was being eroded by hyperinflation.

The representative of **Lebanon** said that the use was required of international accounting standards, as promulgated by the International Accounting Standards Committee (IASC), in the preparation of financial statements by listed banks to provide information to securities exchanges. He emphasized that external auditors needed to develop some way of measuring the inherent risk which banks faced, and that special attention had to be given to transactions between banks and their directors and other related parties. This view was supported by the representative of **Sudan**, who also noted that the lack of sufficient information for the listed banks had weakened the efficiency of the stock market in his country and that banks would be required in the future to report on a quarterly basis.

The representative of **Poland** informed the Group that her country had revised its accounting regulations to bring them into conformity with the European Council's Directives, and that international accounting standards (IASs) were also being used since some of the EC Directives were dated. However, her country was lagging behind in developing rules for new financial instruments. She thought that internal control within banks should be tightened and that guidelines should be developed. This opinion was endorsed by the **Chairperson**, who felt that the Group could provide some guidance in this area and that auditors needed to pay greater attention to internal control measures. The representative of **China** stated that the report on banking was of great use to her country, which was currently formulating accounting and reporting requirements for the banking sector. As China was undergoing economic changes, it had little first-hand experience of some of the pitfalls which could be encountered in a private banking sector. The representative of the **European Commission** said that the EC bank accounts directive contained a good balance between the information shown in the layouts and that contained in the notes. Work was currently under way on accounting and disclosure for new financial instruments. Following the new accounting strategy, the European Union would take into account the work of IASC. The Contact Committee on the Accounting Directives had checked the bank accounts directive against IAS 30 and had found no conflicts.

The representative of **Germany** made the point that the reference in document TD/B/ITNC/AC.1/9 to a "radical change in the business environment for banks" might be correct for some countries. However, it did not seem to reflect the circumstances in Germany and other continental European countries, where under the influence of the prudence principle, the business environment for banks had not changed dramatically. He pointed out further that hidden reserves could be of great use and benefit in times of crisis. Such reserves could extend the opportunities available to banks to provide credits to enterprises. For instance, in the case of the German enterprise "Metallgesellschaft", the Deutsche Bank had been able help ensure that it remained in existence. Finally, market valuations should be discounted by taking into consideration the "value at risk".

The representative of **Brazil** said that a statement on the flow of funds or on cash flows should be one of the required basic financial statements that banks should prepare. The **Chairperson** and the representatives of the **European Commission** and the **Canadian Institute of Chartered Accountants** felt that information on the changes in the components of a bank's shareholders' equity should be provided in the notes to the financial statements rather than constituting a separate basic statement.

The representative of the **European Commission** added that the balance sheet layout should be followed by a line item entitled "off balance sheet items", referring to commitments and contingencies not included in the balance sheet which should be further explained in the notes to the financial statements. The representative of **Lebanon** added that deposits with and from affiliated institutions should be separately reported in the balance sheet.

The representative of **Brazil** expressed the view that a bank's internal accountants and auditors should evaluate the risk management system when evaluating internal controls. Also, a bank's bad debt provisions should not be restricted to the amounts that were deductible for tax reporting purposes but should reflect the true economic conditions that existed. Concerning derivative financial instruments, a bank's disclosures should reflect the purpose for which the transactions were entered into: trading, hedging or speculation. This was the primary information that users of financial statements were seeking in order to evaluate a bank's risk exposure.

A number of delegations and observers commented on the use of hidden reserves. Some felt that such reserves were suitable for enabling banks to stabilize their performance and assisting customers experiencing financial difficulties. This was in conformity with the prudence principle and helped the national economy when significant adverse economic events occurred. A contrasting view was expressed by other delegations, to the effect that the financial statements of banks should be fully transparent, as this added credibility to their financial reporting. Furthermore, reserves should not be used to support the continued existence of potentially insolvent organizations.

A number of comments were made about how banks should measure the various forms of risks in their operations. The representative of the **World Bank** added that internal controls were a very important aspect of a bank's risk management programme. The representative of **Brazil** felt that it was important for a bank to have one worldwide auditor.

The representative of the **International Accounting Standards Committee** (IASC) reported that its Board had approved a reformatted international standard, which became effective in January 1995, on banking disclosures. It had also issued an exposure draft on the presentation of financial statements, which also applied to commercial banks.

Several delegations commented that the supplementary disclosures recommended in the secretariat's report were very useful for consideration by a bank's management, but most of the items were not useful for general reporting purposes and should be reported only to regulatory authorities.

The representative of the **United Kingdom** said that bank supervisors had been making greater use of external auditors in recent years. However, there were other sources of information such as tax authorities. It was important that there be an open relationship between bank supervisors and auditors.

The Group adopted the secretariat's report with amendments and the recommendations in this chapter for disclosure in the balance sheet, profit and loss statement and supplementary information stand for the general guidance of standard-setters.

ISAR agreed that UNCTAD should publish the report (TD/B/ITNC/AC.1/9), with the appropriate amendments, and send it to IASC for its consideration and response.

INTRODUCTION

A. Scope of the chapter

This chapter discusses issues of financial accounting and reporting by commercial banks. It develops guidance for standard-setters with responsibilities for commercial banks. It does not cover commercial and industrial companies or other financial institutions such as insurance companies and securities brokers. However, such companies will find certain recommendations in this chapter both relevant and useful. This is the first time that the Intergovernmental Working Group of Experts considered accounting for commercial banks. However, at its twelfth session it did consider accounting for financial instruments. While no firm conclusions were reached by the Group on appropriate methods to value financial instruments, there was less difficulty in identifying appropriate disclosure rules. These are included in this chapter where relevant, particularly in the discussion of supplementary information which should be disclosed.

B. The expanded role of banks in modern capital markets

Traditionally, commercial banks had the unique role of mobilizing domestic and foreign savings and allocating them among investors. Legislative and regulatory developments in the last decade have radically changed the business environment for banks. Banking deregulation has been both a cause and an effect of the globalization of financial markets. Financial markets in some developed countries have experienced both unprecedented growth and profound structural changes resulting from asset securitization, internationalization and reduced segmentation. Deregulation and innovation have steadily eroded the barriers that have traditionally protected banks from competition. Deposit institutions have been under increasing pressure from competitors offering new products, while at the same time they lost their monopoly over their normal functions owing to increased competition from other financial and non-financial firms. Money markets have seen the development of new types of securities, such as note issuance facilities, euro-commercial paper, certificates of deposit, floating rate notes, notes with various forms of option features, and other complex financial instruments.

In countries with expanding securities markets, the importance of commercial banks as a source of funds to non-financial borrowers has decreased dramatically. Furthermore, even in countries where securities markets are small, banks have still lost loan business because their customers now have increasing access to foreign and offshore capital markets, such as the eurobond market.

Diminishing profits have driven banks either to attempt to maintain their traditional lending activities with expansion into new, riskier areas, such as commercial real-estate and highly leveraged transactions (often bringing in additional concentrations of credit risks); or to pursue riskier, but more profitable off balance sheet activities. Off balance sheet financing has assumed increasing importance for banks because of the pressure of increasingly uniform and stringent capital adequacy requirements. Off balance sheet items were listed in detail in paragraph 42 in Accounting for New Financial Instruments E/C.10/AC.3/1994/5. Among them, interest rate and foreign currency swaps, standby letters of credit, loan commitments, sales and transfers, and guarantees have become major activities for many banks.

A new activity that has generated particular concern recently is the expanding role of banks as dealers in derivatives products. Commercial banks have become users of derivatives not just on behalf of their customers but also to increase the profitability of their operations. Disintermediation has also increased the pressure for legislation to permit banks to expand their services into non-banking activities such as insurance. Although banks are investing in non-banking activities through subsidiaries and other forms of businesses, strict separation between banking and commercial or industrial activities remains the norm, except in countries such as France, Germany and Switzerland.

The cumulative result of the recent developments has been the extensive erosion of the uniqueness of commercial banking. Bank products are becoming increasingly indistinguishable from the products of other financial and non-financial firms. Clearly, the future of banking systems will be the universal banking model prevailing in Europe rather than the highly segmented American and Japanese models. Moreover, banks everywhere are likely to experience a market decline in their role in direct intermediation or asset transformation. Thus, their traditional role of accepting deposits and extending short-term credit will continue to diminish. Instead, they will increase their involvement in indirect intermediation specializing in and servicing capital markets, thus becoming essentially pure information processors. They will probably continue to play a role in payment systems. Furthermore, economies of scale involving information will assume a major role. It can be expected that banks will expand their activities whenever they can take advantage of the joint production of information services, for example in credit card systems, trust activities and insurance.

However, most developing countries, lacking efficient capital markets, will probably continue to rely on financial intermediaries, especially banks, that will maintain their traditional role in economic and monetary systems and within a regulated environment.

C. Accounting and reporting considerations in the new environment of commercial banking

Users of financial statements need to be able to assess the performance of banks not only from the perspective of investors but also from the viewpoint of depositors. Financial institutions have a unique role in the economy as compared with other commercial and industrial enterprises. Whereas the latter have a primary duty to provide information regarding their profitability and solvency to owners, creditors and employees, the former are bound to an even higher fiduciary standard since depositors expect that banks will provide riskless safekeeping for their personal and business wealth. The users of financial statements of commercial banks need to be able to assess solvency, liquidity and profitability. To do this, they need information about the bank's risk exposure and management.

The move towards freer market mechanisms in developed countries is intimately connected with the move to deregulation and less government interference in financial markets. The growing role of the free-market determination of price and quantity in financial markets together with the evolvement of securitization and asset liquidation has created a need for market-based valuations in accounting and/ or reporting by commercial banks and similar financial institutions. Opponents of market-based valuations and accounting argue that it is difficult to make accurate fair-value estimates of assets and liabilities. They claim that historical cost accounting has the important advantage of being easy to apply. On the other hand, proponents of market-value accounting and reporting argue that it alone enables users of financial statements to have an indication of the economic net worth of a bank as well as its exposures to market and credit risks related to certain positions held. The adoption of market value would have the advantage of making a bank's financial condition more transparent. However, since market valuations are volatile, some large banks discount the market value by "value at risk".

At the present time it does not seem that the accounting profession is ready to change from the historical valuation rules for all financial instruments. However, accounting standards which require disclosures based on the fair values of financial instruments have been adopted in several countries as well as by the International Accounting Standards Committee.

With regard to the changed environment necessitating an increasing demand for information about risk exposures and their management, public disclosure would promote market efficiency and discipline. Banks should provide meaningful descriptions of the risks associated with their operating activities, particularly credit risks, concentration of credit risks, interest rate risks, market risks, liquidity risks and other operating risks resulting from on balance sheet and off balance sheet transactions, and a description of their ability to manage these risks. More public information about the risks incurred by banks will better enable users of financial information to evaluate and monitor banks' operations and will act as a deterrent to the taking of excessive risks by their management and directors.

Other important issues concerning commercial banks include the impairment of financial assets and loans, restructurings, hedge accounting and derivative financial instruments, the incorporation of the time value of money into bank accounting, and the sale and transfer of assets. Rapid changes in financial markets and instruments have outstripped the accounting techniques used to measure profitability and risks. In the case of banks, the problems are especially severe and complicate the task of financial reporting, impacting on the reliability of regulatory reports necessary for prudential supervision.

Furthermore, lack of international standardization in the above-mentioned areas has distorted the comparability of the capital positions of international banks. This issue, however, has been taken up in various forums of regulators, for example the Basle Committee. These initiatives reflect the way in which the development of global markets has increased the need for international coordination of regulatory policies and convergence in their content.

I. CURRENT INTERNATIONAL GUIDANCE

Guidance in the area of accounting and disclosures by enterprises generally, and by commercial banks in particular, has been provided by a number of international, regional and national organizations. Persons concerned with accounting and reporting by commercial banks should consider the conceptual frameworks that have been laid down by these organizations for general-purpose reporting to all users of financial statements. These organizations have also recommended accounting principles for matters that apply to enterprises in all economic sectors, for example accounting for retirement benefit costs, leases, and taxes on income, and these should also be taken into consideration. However, commercial banks have unique operations that require special rules for disclosures, regarding for example liquidity, solvency and risks, and these require additional attention.

A description of the international guidance that currently exists follows.

A. Intergovernmental Working Group of Experts on International Standards of Accounting and Reporting

ISAR previously studied the main objectives of general-purpose financial statements and the broad concepts that underlie their preparation and presentation. The results of this study and the recommendations of the Working Group are contained in the publication *Objectives and Concepts Underlying Financial Statements* (New York: United Nations, 1989, Sales No. E.89.II.A.18).

A clear statement of objectives and concepts is useful in formulating national standards on accounting and reporting. The above-mentioned United Nations publication contains information on the objectives of financial statements in providing useful information to all users; the characteristics of useful information; the elemental structure and general concepts underlying financial statements; and comments about some specific components of financial statements. These general accounting principles apply to both financial and non-financial entities.

ISAR has also issued guidance on accounting and reporting for specific matters, which is contained in the publication *Conclusions on Accounting and Reporting by Transnational Corporations* (New York and Geneva: United Nations, 1994, Sales No. E.94.II.A.9). Some of the sections which apply to commercial banks are those dealing with objectives and principles of accounting and reporting; consolidated financial statements; foreign currency transactions and translation; accounting for inflation; disclosure of accounting policies; information items for general-purpose reporting; and contents of the Board of Directors' report.

B. International Accounting Standards Committee

IASC has laid down a framework for the preparation and presentation of financial statements as well as international accounting standards (IASs) on a number of specific accounting and disclosure subjects. IAS 30, Disclosures in the Financial Statements of Banks and Similar Financial Institutions, is particularly relevant to the topic of the present chapter. IAS 32, Financial Instruments: Disclosure and Presentation, a standard issued in 1995, also applies to commercial banks.

C. European Union

The Council of the European Union has issued a directive which relates to accounting and reporting for commercial banks - Council Directive of 8 December 1986 on the Annual Accounts and Consolidated Accounts of Banks and Other Financial Institutions (86/635/EEC). It contains regulations on the layout of bank balance sheets and profit and loss accounts; special provisions with regard to certain items in those financial statements; valuation rules; contents of notes to the accounts; provisions relating to consolidated accounts; and auditing and publication of the accounts.

D. Basle Committee on Banking Supervision

The Basle Committee has been working for a number of years on guidelines for the capital requirements for banks, and this has resulted *inter alia* in the International Convergence of Capital Measurement and Capital Standards (1988) and the Amendment to the Capital Accord to Incorporate Market Risks (1996). More recently, the Basle Committee has been working with the Technical Committee of the International Organization of Securities Commissions (IOSCO) to study banking exposure problems relating to financial derivative transactions. Two documents were jointly issued in 1995 by the Basle Committee and IOSCO:

(1) "Framework for Supervisory Information about the Derivatives Activities of Banks and Securities Firms"; and

(2) "Public Disclosure of the Trading and Derivatives Activities of Banks and Securities Firms".

The first report describes the credit risk, liquidity risk, market risk and earnings information that banks need to develop and disclose concerning their activities in derivatives transactions. It also describes a common minimum information framework which large banks active in the derivatives markets should produce.

The second report, issued later in the year, contains a survey of disclosures in the 1993 and 1994 annual reports of selected banks on their trading and derivatives activities. After comparing the qualitative and quantitative disclosures made, the report makes recommendations for disclosures in future reports by banks and securities firms about their activities in this area.

Considering the importance attached in the financial press in recent years to the significant losses experienced by banks and commercial and industrial companies as a result of transactions in financial derivatives instruments, this guidance as well as guidance from IASC is particularly timely and useful to governments and others interested in bank accounting and disclosure standards.

II. METHODS OF REPORTING BY BANKS TO USERS OF FINANCIAL INFORMATION

A. Annual reports of commercial banks

Annual reports should include the following minimum financial information:

(a)   a balance sheet which summarizes the financial condition of the bank at the reporting date;
(b)   a profit and loss statement which summarizes the income, profits and losses of the bank resulting from its operations for the reporting period;
(c)   notes to the financial statements which constitute an integral part thereof; notes should contain a report on the shareholders' equity which describes the changes in its components, including

the permanent capital, retained earnings and capital reserves accounts. In certain countries the practice is to separate the report on changes in shareholders' equity from the report on changes in retained earnings;

    (d)   a statement by the board of directors; and

    (e)   an auditor's opinion on the statements based upon his or her examination.

The financial reports are historical documents (usually drawn up on the basis of the accounting convention of historical costs) and they contain mostly financial data. In some countries adjustments for the effects of inflation might be included. The information reported sometimes reflects estimates and professional valuations, as well as asset and liability evaluations made by the management of the reporting entity.

To increase the reliability of the reports and to strengthen the confidence of the users in the information contained therein, it is essential that the annual financial statements be examined by an impartial auditor. Information that accompanies the financial reports but does not constitute an integral part thereof may also be examined by the auditors in order to confirm that it does not contain misleading items or items that substantially contradict the information contained in the financial statements.1 The subject of auditing is discussed further in a later section of this chapter.

B. Basic financial statements

1. Balance sheet

The balance sheet, also referred to as the statement of condition or the statement of financial position, is a report which shows the financial position of an institution at a specific time, including its financial or other economic resources, other assets, obligations, liabilities, and the residual claims of the shareholders - the shareholders' equity. The balance sheet, together with the other financial statements, is designed to reflect the state of liquidity and solvency of the bank and the relative level of risk, including transaction concentrations relating to the various assets and liabilities accounts. Thus the main division into sections of the balance sheet is by the nature of the assets and liabilities.

However, like all financial satements, the balance sheet has limitations as regards its usefulness because it reports on the accounts of the bank only as of a specific date. The more current conditions in an institution could change dramatically in a very short period of time because of the nature of its operations.

The balance sheet of a bank is usually drawn up in descending order of liquidity, but the classification is not into current and non-current assets. The reason for this is that the special nature of banking activities and banking products renders such classifications meaningless. However, for purposes of measurement, it is necessary to distinguish between on the one hand, fixed (or tangible) and intangible assets and assets held for "investment", and financial assets held to maturity, and on the other hand assets intended to be realized in the near future - such as loans held for sale, securities held for short-term profit-making and real-estate held for sale.

The normal reporting procedure is to present the previous year's data in comparable figures in the balance sheet and in the relevant notes.

2. Balance sheet account classifications

It is recommended that the following major account titles be reported in a commercial bank's balance sheet:

ASSETS

*   Cash and balances with central banks
*   Treasury bills and other bills eligible for refinancing with central banks
*   Deposits with other banks
*   Securities
*   Loans and advances[2]
*   Investment in affiliates and participating interests
*   Other assets (including tangible and intangible assets)
*   Accrued interest receivable
*   Total assets

LIABILITIES AND SHAREHOLDERS' EQUITY

*   **Liabilities**
*   Deposits from banks
*   Other deposits[3]
*   Debt evidenced by certificates
*   Other liabilities
*   Accrued interest payable
*   Provisions for liabilities and charges
*   Subordinated liabilities
*   Total liabilities
*   Minority interests
*   In-substance capital liabilities
*   **Shareholders' equity**
    -   Paid-up share capital
    -   Reserves
    -   Retained earnings
    -   Total shareholders' equity
*   Total liabilities and shareholders' equity
*   Off balance sheet items, including commitments and contingent liabilities

In addition, the body of the balance sheet should include a comment that the notes to the financial statements constitute an integral part of them.

The above format is suitable, with appropriate modifications, for either a consolidated or a separate legal entity balance sheet.

3. Comments on certain balance sheet items

General

In some countries it is customary to provide greater detail within the balance sheet sections. In other countries it is optional to present certain details either in the body of the balance sheet or in the notes. The approach recommended in this chapter is not to overburden the body of the balance sheet with excessive details, but instead to provide the required disclosures in the notes. This approach is the accepted practice in, for example, the United States and the United Kingdom, although there are certain differences in the types of items appearing in the body of the balance sheet in different countries, which arise from differences in the structure of the banking, financial and capital markets of those countries.

The format above presents a uniform and broad structure for banking systems that differ in their legal and regulatory environments, as well as in the level of financial services, the degree of development of the markets, and the economic-business environment. Naturally, the presentation is subject to the rules of substantiveness, and it is possible in principle to combine several non-substantive sections and present them as a single section. Nevertheless, in presenting a format for wide use it is felt that such combinations will be rare in a normal bank with a wide range of operating activities.

A bank may present additional items in its balance sheet using the above format, either as sub-divisions of the above items or by creating additional sections for items not covered. Such items may also be included in sections entitled above as "other assets" or "other liabilities", with additional disclosures in the footnotes.

In-substance capital liabilities

In-substance capital liabilities include amounts for financial instruments that are equity instruments issued by the bank (capital) according to their economic nature but which cannot legally be considered part of shareholders' equity. The distinction between equity instruments and liability instruments is described in IAS 32, which states that:

"The substance of a financial instrument, rather than its legal form, governs its classification on the issuer's balance sheet. While substance and legal form are commonly consistent, this is not always the case. For example, some financial instruments take the legal form of equity but are liabilities in substance and others may combine features associated with equity instruments and features associated with financial liabilities. The classification continues at each subsequent reporting date until the financial instrument is removed from the enterprise's balance sheet."[4]

As a consequence, instruments which, from the point of view of their legal form, are equity instruments, although in economic substance are debt instruments, should be included in an appropriate liabilities section. A footnote should be included that details the relevant amounts in order to clarify the accounting treatment of these types of instruments.

4. Profit and loss accounts (income statement)

The profit and loss statement of a bank is unique in that it presents financing as the main operating activity and details the various components of the income and expenses (interest) separately from those arising from other operating activities. Furthermore, as in all enterprises, the results of a bank's current activities are separated from results obtained from investments (as part of its ongoing activities) and from non-current or non-regular activities.

The report should normally be drawn up on a consolidated basis and include comparative figures for the previous year. There are two generally accepted methods for drawing up the profit and loss account: the horizontal method and the vertical method. The latter is generally prevalent in the United States, the United Kingdom and other countries. The Council of Europe's Directive permits the use of either method, without a preference for one or the other. It is common practice to note data on the designation of profits in the margins as the "retained profit account" (United Kingdom) or the "retained earnings report" (United States). However, the most appropriate place for this information is in the report on changes in shareholders' equity (see below for further comments).

The initial classification of income and expenses in the profit and loss account should be by type, and not by source. Additional information classifying the income and expenses by source, with direct reference to the assets and liabilities sections, should be given in the notes. Offsetting (netting) of income and expense items is not appropriate unless it relates to hedges and to assets and liabilities which have been offset in the balance sheet. Profits and losses from trading activities such as securities and foreign exchange, and profits and losses from realizing investment securities, can be presented on a net basis. This is discussed further in a later section of this chapter.

Overall, the main body of the report should not be overburdened with information, and additional details and clarifications should appear as footnotes.

5. Profit and loss account classifications

It is recommended that the following major account titles be reported by commercial banks in profit and loss statements:

Net interest income
* Interest receivable and similar income
* Dividend income from investments
* Interest payable and similar charges
* Provisions for credit losses
* Net interest revenue after provision for credit losses

Non-interest income
* Fees and commissions receivable
* Net trading account (dealing) profits (losses)
* Net realized gains on sales of investment securities
* Net realized gains from sale of loans
* Other operating income
* Income from investments in associated companies
* Gains from disposal of investments in group companies

Non-interest expenses
* Salaries and employee benefits
* Depreciation and amortization
* Other occupancy expenses
* Fees and commissions payable
* Deposit insurance premiums
* Other operating charges
* Amounts written off on investments
* Losses on termination and disposal of group operations
* Group profits on ordinary activities (before taxes)
* Taxes on group profits
* Profits on ordinary activities after taxes
* Minority interests
* Group profit before extraordinary items

Extraordinary items and accumulated effect of change in accounting methods

Net profit (loss)
Profit per share
- primary
- fully diluted

7. Notes to the financial statements

It is not practicable to describe in detail all the items that should be included in the notes to the financial statements. Specifications on some matters are contained in the sections below entitled "Supplementary financial data" and "Supplementary information". Following is a brief listing of the main topics that should be considered for disclosure in the footnotes:

(a)   Summary of significant accounting policies, including the basis of consolidation, i.e. a description of how the assets, liabilities, profits and losses of subsidiaries have been treated in the group accounts; accounting policies relating to investments and bad and doubtful debts; adjustments for inflation; foreign currency translation adjustments; taxes on income, etc.;

(b)   Cash and balances with central banks, including restrictions on cash;

(c)   Treasury bills and other bills eligible for refinancing with central banks;

(d)   Deposits in other banks;

(e)   Securities;

(f)   Loans and advances;

(g)   Allowance for bad and doubtful debts:

(h)   Investments in affiliated enterprises;

(i)   Premises and equipment;

(j)   Other assets;

(k)   Foreclosed assets;

(l)   Securities purchased under resale agreements;

(m)   Sales and repurchase transactions;

(n)   Loans sold with recourse;

(o)   Leases;

(p)   Deferred assets;

(q)   Liens and other restrictive conditions;

(r)   Deposits from banks;

(s)   Other deposits;

(t)   Debts evidenced by certificates;

(u)   Other liabilities;

(v)   Provision for liabilities and charges;

(w)   Subordinated liabilities;

(x)   In-substance capital liabilities;

(y)   Shareholders' equity;

(z)   Reserves;

(aa)   Dividends paid, payable and proposed;

(ab)   Earning per share, including the basis of the calculation;

(ac)   Statutory and regulatory requirements, including capital requirements;

(ad)   Details of interest income and expenses by source;

(ae)   Dividend income from investments;

(af)   Non-interest income;

(ag)   Salaries and employee benefits costs;

(ah)   Pension schemes and details of their financing;

(ai)   Post-retirement benefit plans;

(aj)   Extraordinary profit and loss items;

(ak)   Details of the current and deferred taxation provisions;

(al)   Commitments and contingencies;

(am)   Off balance sheet credit risks;

(an)   Off balance sheet financial instruments, including derivatives;

(ao)   Concentrations of credit risks;

(ap) Concentrations of other assets and liabilities;

(aq) Non-performing loans and other troubled debts;

(ar) Maturities of assets, liabilities and off balance sheet items;

(as) Fair value and other information concerning financial instruments;

(at) Reporting by geographical and business segments;

(au) Related party disclosures, including related party transactions, interests in transactions and holdings, directors' emoluments, etc.;

(av) Trust activities;

(aw) Management and agency services;

(ax) List of principal subsidiaries, and other significant group holdings;

(ay) Government assistance;

(az) Parent company separate reports (unconsolidated);

(aaa) Statement on changes in shareholders' equity

In order to report changes in the equity of the bank, the capital accounts should be classified and presented in the following groups:

*   Paid-up share capital
*   Receipts on account of shares and receipts from options
*   Premiums on share purchases
*   Revaluation funds
*   Funds reserved for redeeming shares
*   Currency translation differentials
*   Other funds (such as options and rights that have expired)
*   Total share paid-up capital and capital funds
*   Surpluses (deficits)
*   Total shareholders' equity
*   In-substance capital liabilities
*   Total shareholders' equity and in-substance capital liabilities

The report on changes in shareholders' equity will present the amounts at the beginning of the year, the amounts at the end of the year, and transactions that occurred during the year separately for each component of the shareholders' equity accounts listed above. Amounts as of the beginning of the year and the end of the year for items which by law belong to the capital group but which by virtue of their economic nature were classified in the liabilities section will be noted as such. In the event of limitations on the distribution of surpluses and funds distributable as cash, notes will be made concerning the sums, the nature of the limitations, the period of the limitations and their conditions.

8. Consolidated financial statements

The financial statements of a banking enterprise should be presented in a consolidated format using an appropriate methodology. If a subsidiary of a banking corporation has been acquired with the intention of its being disposed of in the near future, for example a bank whose shares are being held temporarily as a result of a financial assistance operation with a view to its reorganization, the annual accounts of the subsidiary should be attached to the consolidated accounts and additional information given in the notes to the accounts concerning the nature and terms of the financial assistance operation.

9. Level of disclosure and exemption from disclosure

One of the problems in financial reporting for banks is deciding the appropriate level of disclosures that should be made. In this respect, banking confidentiality and maintaining the financial stability of the institution weigh heavily on decisions that are taken. Certain countries have introduced into their regulations guidelines which enable the banks to refrain from disclosing sensitive information that is likely to derogate from confidentiality or which reflects on the ability of the banks to obtain deposits. In Germany and Switzerland, for example, banks have the right not to disclose the provisions for doubtful debts and the market value of their investments. In the United States, on the other hand, the approach is one of full disclosure of the business situation of the institution, including a description of its management of risks, information on interest rate differentials, allowances for doubtful debts, debts restructured and other problem debts, the market value of assets and liabilities, activity and exposures according to business and geographical sectors, credit concentrations, and many other matters.

Regardless of whether an item is explicitly required to be disclosed according to national regulations, all items of information should be detailed and any clarification should be given if:

(a)   because of their absence the financial reports do not give a true and fair view of the business condition of the banking enterprise at the balance sheet date, the results of its activities for the reporting period, and the changes in its shareholders' equity; and

(b)   the disclosures are required in order to ensure that the financial report or any part of it will not be misleading to readers.

A banking institution may add to the disclosure requirements but should not detract from them.

C. Supplementary financial data

The supplementary financial data are intended to support and complete the information contained in the financial statements by analysing and focusing attention on a number of key issues. When the bank issues consolidated financial statements the data should be presented on a consolidated basis. Specific items that are recommended for disclosure include:

(a)   Development trends:
    (i)   a five-year summary balance sheet and profit and loss account, and comparative selected ratios for this period:
        -     per share data, including average common shares outstanding
        -     profitability ratios
        -     capital ratios
        -     other data, such as number of employees at the end of each period
    (ii)   interim periods - financial statements for the four quarters of the year with comparative figures for the previous year;

(b)   Analysis of financing (interest) income and expenses to enable the user to compare the bank's performance in the financing area with comparable figures of its competitors. These data also enable the user to isolate and analyse factors affecting interest income and expenses;

(c)   Information on interest rate risk. The disclosure described in IAS 32 is as follows:

"Information about maturity dates, or repricing dates when they are earlier, indicates the length of time for which interest rates are fixed and information about effective interest rates indicates the levels at which they are fixed. Disclosure of this information provides financial statement users with a basis for evaluating the interest rate price risk to which an enterprise is exposed and thus the potential for gains or losses. For instruments that reprice to a market rate of interest before maturity, disclosure of the period until the next repricing is more important than disclosure of the period to maturity."[5]

The measurement of interest rate risk is still undecided and is the focus of the work of the Basle Committee and other regulators.

(d)   Foreign exchange risk and liquidity - the distribution of assets and liabilities according to their nominated currency and contractual maturities;

(e)   Credit risks, including concentrations, credits to foreign countries, credit risks of off balance sheet items, information about troubled debts, and an analysis of the allowance for bad and doubtful debts, including movements in the allowance during the course of the year;

(f)   Details of substantial concentrations of liabilities.

D. Report by the management and directors

Management and directors should explain the nature of their responsibility for preparing the reports in a statement that would normally be presented before the auditor's report. Issues such as the following should be addressed:

(a)   The legal requirements for management and directors to prepare financial reports that truly and fairly reflect the state of the bank's business and the outcomes of its activities;

(b)   The responsibility of management and directors to keep true and fair accounts, to preserve the organization's assets, and to prevent and disclose embezzlement, fraud and other infractions;

(c)   A declaration that proper accounting rules, implemented consistently and supported by conservative considerations and evaluations, were used in preparing the financial reports;

(d)   A declaration that the reports were prepared according to generally accepted accounting principles and that any departure from these was disclosed and explained in the notes;

(e)   A declaration that the reports were examined by independent auditors who received all the information and cooperation they needed in order to make their examination and prepare their report;

(f)   A declaration that management maintains a proper system of internal control throughout the year and exercises care that its actions taken were in accordance with all relevant laws, rules and regulations to which the bank is subject in order to preserve its safety and security;

(g)   Management's evaluation of the effectiveness of the internal control structure and the internal control procedures; and

(h)   A statement that the organization is a going concern, with supporting evidence or assumptions, as necessary.

Any area in which there is a deviation should be noted, with details of the reasons for the deviation being given. The statement should be signed by the chairman of the board of directors, the general manager of the bank (the chief executive officer), and the senior officer directly responsible for the preparation of the accounts.

E. Supplementary information

Management should carefully consider what supplementary information is relevant and needs to be disclosed to the public using the materiality test. It could provide a supplementary report with information concerning any events, trends or uncertainties which will have a substantial impact on the financial state of the bank or on the results of its operations. The information should be in the historical context but with a future perspective. Whereas the financial statements of the bank are based on historical data or some other basis of accounting, the purpose of the supplementary financial information is to give a forward perspective and management's point of view. This part of the report should be the link between financial statements that give the results of past business activities and the external decision-makers who are trying to ascertain the bank's future. Regulators in the United States, for example, follow such principles.[6]

Specific reference should be made to issues or developments which, at the reporting date, have a very great likelihood of occurring. Also, estimates should be provided of the results that could occur if and when the developments materialize. The discussion of such matters is supposed to be read in conjunction with the basic financial statements and the supplementary financial data, and is designed to amplify, augment and otherwise enhance the understanding of the substance of the information contained in the financial statements. The discussion should analyse what happened, why it happened, the implications for the bank's liquidity, capital adequacy, resources and operations, and how the event(s) may or may not be a consequence of events in the past periods, or is indicative of what may happen in future periods.

Information and developments in the bank's main areas of activities, its operations in business and geographical cross-sections, and developments during the course of the reporting periods should be disclosed. Five broad aspects of the bank's business should be addressed:

(i)   the results of operations and the bank's profitability;
(ii) capital resources;
(iii) short-term and long-term liquidity;
(iv) capital adequacy, asset quality and risk management; and
(v)   information concerning directors and senior officers of the bank.

Information on substantial changes from one year to the next in the financial reporting sections, changes in accounting or valuations policies, and other effects of accounting measurement methods on the presentation of the business results and the financial situation can greatly enhance the reliability of the basic financial statements. However, the supplementary financial information should be interpretative and insightful and not merely reiterate the numerical data contained in the financial statements, nor merely recite the changes from year to year which can be readily computed from the financial statements. The information a user expects to find in this report need not reveal specific business transactions, specific clients or privy information of the bank.

The following details should be disclosed, to the extent that they are relevant and material, and may be reported upon using the data included in the financial statements, the supplementary financial data and any additional sources known to management:

(a)   Information regarding management's handling of current issues, in order to characterize the bank's operations during the reporting period;

(b)   Information obtained by management regarding trends or phenomena that are currently identifiable and that may significantly affect the bank's financial position and results of operations. This includes subjects or developments that are likely to occur and the expected specific influences that the matters should have on the bank. Reference should be made to events that occurred both before and after the balance sheet date and which will influence the bank as well as its subsidiary companies;

(c)   Significant differences, from year to year, in the financial statement items if the explanations are conducive to understanding the bank's overall business operations. The explanations should include reference to those quantitative factors which explain the changes;

(d)   Explanations of significant matters which the bank's external auditor sets forth in his or her report;

(e)   Description of unusual developments during interim periods in the reporting year which caused operations to fluctuate disproportionately;

(f)   Explanations for unusual accelerated remittances on assets or repayments of liabilities during the year, noting the estimated volume of the accelerated amounts and the principal changes in the terms and conditions of the items for which the remittances and repayments were accelerated;

(g)   Unusual fluctuations in income and expense accounts, including reference to tax expenses and irregular transactions and their effect on the group's net profits. Reference should be made to the bank's and the consolidated group's profitability using relevant ratios and measures that explain return on capital, income components, factors that influence net profits, efficiency in utilizing resources, and so forth;

(h)   Average rates of income earned on financial assets, the average expense rates on liabilities and the interest gaps or margins, including a reference to the volume and price effects on interest income and expenses;

(i)   The effect of provisions for doubtful and bad debts and the amount of doubtful and bad debts collected during the period;

(j)   The structure of the group's assets and liabilities, including comments about core and non-core business activities;

(k)   Details of significant changes in the portfolio of real estate held by the bank and its subsidiaries, and the difference between the book values and the market values of these assets at the end of the year;

(l)   Particulars regarding investment activities, especially those investments carried at an amortized cost:

  (i)   If the market value of the portfolio is lower than its book value, an evaluation should be made of the implications of the imputed loss for the bank's net worth and capital requirements;

  (ii) An analysis and quantification should be made of the expected effects on current net profits, future net profits, return on investment, liquidity and financing as a result of:
        - significant unrealized losses in the portfolio;
        - significant sales of securities at a profit; and
        - significant changes in the average maturity of the investments.
        A similar analysis should be performed in cases where a significant portion of fixed interest mortgage loans with maturity dates of more than one year bear lower interest rates than the current interest rate;

  (iii) If significant unplanned sales were made from the investment portfolio, the report should describe those transactions which were not forecast in the past and which caused management to modify its investment strategy. The fact that this possibility was not predicted in disclosures of previous years may need to be highlighted;

  (iv) If a significant portion of the portfolio includes securities that are not actively traded in a liquid market, the report should disclose these and describe their nature and the source of information used to determine their market value. Each significant risk related to the investment vis-à-vis profitability and liquidity should be discussed. If the portfolio is composed of financial instruments with an especially volatile market value and if this volatility may significantly harm business results or liquidity, appropriate disclosures should be made.

(m)   The status of the bank's capital resources and any changes therein, including capital issues and dividend distributions and information on declared dividend amounts in the current year and the prior year;

(n)   A description of the risks to which the bank is exposed and a description of the bank's risk management principles and methods. Reference should also be made to the various risk ratios which the bank has developed and specific details of the means used by the bank to measure and manage risks. A separate reference should be made to:

(i)   credit risks;
(ii) price risks;
(iii) interest rate risks;
(iv) currency and market risks;
(v)   market liquidity risks and funding risks;
(vi) governmental/political risks (including country risks);
(vii) operational risks; and
(viii) any other relevant risks that may have a significant bearing on the bank's activities and the results of its operations.

In this framework references should be made, *inter alia*, to provisions for doubtful debts, the credit risks of on balance sheet and off balance sheet items, significant credit concentrations, collateral policies and the types of collateral vis-à-vis different types of credit. Also, reference should be made to:

(i)   collection activities and amounts which are in the process of collection;
(ii) specification of credit exposures by business segments and countries;
(iii) an analysis of the repayment periods and the duration of assets and liabilities;
(iv) the fair value of assets and liabilities; and
(v)   other relevant information.

(o)   An analysis by business segment of income and expenses incurred by the group and details of assets and liabilities in each segment, together with developments that have occurred in the operations of each segment;

(p)   A description of the geographical distribution of the bank's operating locations outside its headquarters, noting the branches in foreign countries. The major developments at the locations during the reporting period should be described. An analysis by geographical segments should be made of the income and expenses of the group, with specifications of assets and liabilities and related significant developments;

(q)   Activities of the group's main associated companies, including significant developments in their assets, liabilities, income and expenses. The group's return on its investments in these companies should also be disclosed;

(r)   The effects on the bank's business results of major developments in the banking industry, both locally and abroad. Background data on local and worldwide economic and legislative developments should be provided if relevant. Reference should be made as necessary to matters of supervision and compliance with regulatory requirements;

(s)   Details regarding transactions with related parties which were not conducted at "arm's length", and any significant transactions that were conducted after the balance date or for which there are intentions to enter into such transactions;

(t)   Information on off balance sheet activities such as trustee, proxy, agent, dealership or managerial operations. The bank's involvement with financial instruments and the group's non-banking activities should also be disclosed. If the bank or its subsidiaries took part in trust activities, these should be described, along with the associated income related to them, by type of trust;

(u)   Discussion of the bank's liquidity, and the management's policy for raising resources;

(v)   Changes in the bank's organizational structure, including branches and personnel, and a review of related policies and plans. Disclosure should be provided as to the number of employees and any employment agreements. These employment data should be presented, by operating activity in the local and foreign markets;

(w)   A diagram or list of the group's holdings in other corporations and a description of the respective capital interests and voting rights (or right to appoint directors);

(x)   The names of all the directors of the bank who held office during the year. Additional information concerning the directors who were in office at the end of the year should be provided, for instance their principal occupations, other organizations in which they hold offices or in which they are members of the board of directors, and the unexpired period of the service contract of each director proposed for re-election. The independent external directors of the bank must be identified and a short biography of each provided. The names of the members of the Compensation and Audit Committees should be given.

(y)   The names of senior management, and the position and compensation (including salary and benefits) of each, received either directly or indirectly during the year from the bank and its subsidiaries;

(z)   The number of meetings held by the board of directors during the reported year;

(aa)   The emoluments and other benefits paid or provided directly or indirectly by the bank or its subsidiaries to the chairman of the board of directors separately, and to all other directors as a whole;

(ab)   Any sums loaned or guaranteed by the bank or its subsidiaries in favour of the bank's directors;

(ac)   Details of the interests of directors and senior managers and their immediate families in significant agreements that were concluded during the year, or that are in force at the end of the year, to which the bank or one of its subsidiaries is a party. If no such agreements exist, a statement to this effect should be included;

(ad)   The financial interests of the directors and senior management in shares, debentures, options and convertible securities of the group. The report should distinguish between beneficial and non-beneficial interests;

(ae)   A declaration as to whether the bank has purchased insurance for directors, officers, employees or auditors against liabilities related to the bank's activities;

(af)   Details regarding the acquisition of the bank's own shares during the year, or possession of the bank's own shares in any other manner. The following details should be noted:

>   (i)   number and nominal sum of the shares;
>   (ii)   their portion of the paid-in capital;
>   (iii)   cost paid and the reason for the acquisition or circumstances of the transfer of ownership to the bank;
>   (iv)   shares that were cancelled or sold during the year;

(ag)   Disclosure of donations to political persons, entities and other bodies by the bank and its subsidiaries if the amount is significant;

(ah)   Description of the character and the extent of current or expected governmental financial aid and its effect on the bank's financial position and results of its operations;

(ai)   Presentation of all other data that, in the opinion of the board of directors and management, could be of importance to the users of the report in order to clarify the state of affairs of the bank and its subsidiaries and to prevent misleading interpretations.

III. SPECIFIC ACCOUNTING AND REPORTING MATTERS

A. Measurement of interest income and expenses

The method of recognizing income and expenses from interest-bearing assets and liabilities, excluding non-performing assets, is known as the "interest method". Other methods of recognizing income can be used only to the extent that they constitute a true and fair approximation of the interest method. This method calculates interest on the basis of the effective yield, using the outstanding balances of the respective assets or liabilities accounts. The amortization of premiums and discounts should be calculated on an actuarial basis so as to produce a level yield over the period to maturity. A straight line method may be used only if it does not materially distort the reported profits. The amounts of remaining unamortized premiums or discounts must be disclosed in the notes to the accounts.

The most common practice followed is to disclose the balance of the cumulative interest receivable and payable in the balance sheet under separate headings within the assets and liabilities sections. Alternatively, the balances could be added to the assets or liabilities from which they are derived, but this is not the recommended practice. The amounts of interest paid or received during the operating period covered by the report and, for comparative amounts, from preceding periods should be presented separately within the "other assets" and "other liabilities" classifications.

B. Netting of amounts

1. Balance sheet netting

In many countries, for example in the European Union, netting is prohibited, even for debit and credit balances for the same customer. For example, in the United Kingdom it is forbidden to net assets and liabilities as well as to net income and expenses.[7]   However, debit and credit balances should be netted if they truly are not separate assets and liabilities. This should also be followed for the economic reality of certain of the new financial instruments that have emerged in recent years. Nevertheless, there are differences in the netting conditions permitted in certain countries. Generally, the conditions for netting are as follows:

(a)   The reporting entity and the other party owe each other a determinable monetary sum denominated in the same currency or another exchangeable currency;

(b)   The reporting entity can impose a net settlement for completing the transaction; and,

(c)   The capability of the entity or person as stated in part (b) to complete the transaction is assured beyond any reasonable doubt and there is no chance that the reporting entity will be required to pay its liability without realizing the related asset.

A British Bankers' Association Statement of Recommended Practice (SORP) on accounting for advances recommends the implementation of netting only when there is a legal and enforceable right of netting between accounts in the event of the liquidation of the other party and only when there are no circumstances beyond the control of the banking entity that are likely to impede its ability to realize the right recovery of the asset involved in the transaction. The EC banking directive (see section I.C. above) does not deal with this issue for the balance sheet but does require it for the profit and loss account (see paragraph 64). However, the criterion adopted by the IAS 32 states that:

"A financial asset and a financial liability should be offset and the net amount reported in the balance sheet when an enterprise: (a) has a legally enforceable right to set off the recognised amounts; and (b) intends either to settle on a net basis or to realise the asset and settle the liability simultaneously."[8]

The standard requires the presentation of financial assets and financial liabilities on a net basis when this reflects an enterprise's expected future cash flows from settling two or more separate financial instruments. When an enterprise has the right to receive or pay a single net amount and intends to do so, it has in effect only a single financial asset or liability. In other circumstances, financial assets or financial liabilities should be presented separately from each other, consistent with their characteristics as resources or obligations of the enterprise.

IAS 32 permits netting between amounts from different customers when there is an agreement between the bank and the two parties to this effect.[9]   Finally, the IAS also allows netting under conditions of a "master netting arrangement", in which more than two parties are involved.[10]

2. *Profit and loss account netting*

The recommended policy for the netting of amounts in the profit and loss statement is the one promulgated by IASC in IAS 30. This standard states that:

"(a) netting is permitted in the profit and loss accounts where it is permitted between the relevant assets and liabilities in the balance sheet because a legal right of offset exists and the offsetting represents the expectation as to the realization or settlement of the asset or liability; or where (b) the income and expenses are netted as a result of the implementation of hedge accounting."[11]

Article 32 of the EC banking directive allows netting in three cases.

C. Reserves

1. *Reserves for general banking risks*

The EC banking directive permits the creation of a reserve for general banking risks, as a liability item, and requires the creation of such a reserve in the case of application of the option of downward revaluation of assets on the grounds of conservatism (Article 38). IAS 30 permits the creation of reserves for general banking risks, including future losses or other risks not yet identified; however, the reserve is not to appear in the profit and loss account but is to be registered directly as an adjustment of surpluses which will be presented separately.

It is recommended that care be taken that the creation of reserves for general banking risks does not become an instrument for manipulating and smoothing profits which would derogate from the ability of users of information to compare the financial condition and performance of banks.

2. *Hidden reserves*

Many governmental authorities and other persons assert that hidden reserves should be maintained in the interest of security for depositors. The position is that hidden reserves enable a bank to achieve stability of its reported profits by transfers to and from these reserves. Hidden reserves can be created in two ways: by maintaining an internal reserve, and by a downward revaluation of assets.

The EC banking directive[12] gives member countries the option of a downward revaluation of certain assets of up to 4 per cent of their worth before revaluation. These assets are neither held as financial fixed assets nor included in a trading portfolio. This option is applied by five countries and rejected by ten. Its suitability is currently under discussion.

It is recommended that reserves or provisions for losses on assets be created only in accordance with the economic substance of events that have occurred and not as a means of providing hidden reserves. Depreciation and amortization should be recorded only in accordance with accepted methods and rates.

D. Disclosures about derivative financial instruments

In 1994 the Intergovernmental Working Group of Experts on International Standards of Accounting and Reporting (ISAR) studied the subject of accounting for the relatively new types of financial instruments and their report is included in the publication *International Accounting and Reporting Issues*: 1994 (New York and Geneva: United Nations, 1995, Sales No. E.95.II.A3), pp. 61-69). In 1995 the International Accounting Standards Committee published International Accounting

Standard 32, Financial Instruments: Disclosure and Presentation. In addition, the European Council, the Basle Committee on Banking Supervision, the British Bankers' Association and the United States Financial Accounting Standards Board, among others, have published guidance in this area.

IAS 32 requires information to be furnished for all financial instruments regarding their extent and nature, including significant terms and conditions that could affect the amounts, their timing and the certainty of future cash flows. It states that banks should disclose the essential characteristics of the instruments, referring to proper grouping of similar instruments. When financial instruments expose the enterprise to significant risks, IAS 32 requires that the following information be disclosed:

(a)   the instruments' principal, stated, face and notional amounts, maturities, options that are related, and cash flow characteristics; and

(b)   information about interest rate risks, including data about off balance sheet instruments.

Furthermore, IAS 32 states that where there is a relationship between financial instruments that could affect the enterprise's normal cash flow, such as in hedging transactions, it is important to disclose the relationships that exist and the enterprise's exposures to risk.

The Basle Committee and the IOSCO Technical Committee encourage banks to provide meaningful summary information on their trading and derivatives activities. Disclosures should provide a picture of the scope and nature of an institution's trading and derivatives activities, as well as information on the major risks associated with these activities, including credit risk, market risk and liquidity risk. Furthermore, institutions should disclose information on the actual performance in managing these risks, particularly with regard to exposure to market risk. For fundamental disclosures of an institution's derivatives activities, institutions are encouraged to use the common minimum framework. This lists the different types of risks (credit, liquidity, market, earnings) and describes what should be disclosed.

E. Concentration of transactions

An important disclosure that should be made by commercial banks concerns information relating to concentrations of their transactions. Appropriate guidance is given in IAS 30, paragraphs 41 and 42, as follows:

"A bank [should disclose] significant concentrations in the distribution of its assets and in the source of its liabilities because it is a useful indication of the potential risks inherent in the realisation of the assets and the funds available to the bank. Such disclosures are made in terms of geographical areas, customer or industry groups or other concentrations of risk which are appropriate in the circumstances of the bank. A similar analysis and explanation of off balance sheet items is also important. Geographical areas may include individual countries, groups of countries or regions within a country. Customer disclosures may deal with sectors such as governments, public authorities, and commercial and business enterprises..."

The disclosure of significant net foreign currency exposures is also a useful indication of the risk of losses arising from changes in exchange rates.

F. Trust estates and collateralized assets

A business transaction conducted by a banking institution in trust for a third party, an asset held by an organization such as a trust estate or assets that others have collateralized in the bank's favour should not be presented in the financial statements unless such assets are cash in hand which mingles with the totality of the bank's activities. Such an asset can be netted against the corresponding liability part of the transaction for a depositor of the guarantee if the netting criteria have been met (see the section on netting above). An exception can be made in the case of collateralized assets which are, in substance, a foreclosure according to the accounting rules. In this case, they will be presented in the "other assets" section of the balance sheet.

IV. BANK AUDITING

In almost all countries the accounts of banks are examined by an independent auditor. These examinations tend to be of two types: those where the auditor concentrates on whether the accounts are properly prepared in accordance with national laws and regulations, and those where there has been a more thorough review and examination of the business and individual transactions to ensure that the financial statements reflect a true and fair view of the banks' state of affairs and the results of its operations.

It should be emphasized that the objective of an audit examination of a bank, as for enterprises in any other economic sector, is not primarily to prevent business failures but to render an opinion on the fairness of the financial statements. In carrying out their role, independent auditors of a bank should be aware of the general business and economic risk factors that affect the industry as well as the specific operating features of banks that may cause special problems. In particular, the auditor must be aware that:

(a) Banks have custody of large volumes of money and other easily liquidated instruments whose physical security has to be ensured. This applies to both the storage and the transfer of money, and it makes banks vulnerable to misappropriations and frauds. Therefore, banks need to establish, implement and enforce rigorous systems of internal control and operating procedures;

(b) Banks engage in large volumes and varieties of transactions both in terms of number and value. This necessitates complex accounting and internal control systems and extensive dependence on computerized systems to process transactions;

(c) Auditors of banks should give particular attention to the assessment of the possibility that financial assets might be impaired as well as other risks involving financial instruments;

(d) Banks usually have wide geographical dispersion, including establishments in foreign countries. This necessarily involves a greater decentralization of authority and dispersal of accounting and control functions with consequent difficulties in maintaining uniformity of compliance with organizational policies and operating controls. Following are some of the factors that have to be considered:

(i)   Banks frequently engage in significant off balance sheet activities that may not involve accounting entries and might not leave an audit trail;

(ii)   Banks are regulated by governmental authorities and regulatory requirements which often influence accounting and auditing practices. Non-compliance with regulatory requirements could have significant implications for the banks' financial viability;

(iii) Banks are frequently very vulnerable to abuses through related party transactions because of the easy access to cash and because of the large flows of funds in a bank's operations. Particularly in international operations, banks are frequently exposed to a large number of related parties. Identifying all related parties may be very difficult and may cost more than the benefits acknowledged by users of financial statements. Also, the growing complexity of transactions makes it difficult to trace the terms and conditions of transactions with related parties that were not executed in the ordinary course of business.

As a result of the industry's particular features, the auditors of banks face greater audit risks. Developments during the last decade have made their work even more difficult. In this respect, deregulation, institutionalization and globalization have had three significant impacts on bank auditing risks:

(a)   Inherent risks: auditors face a non-consistent business environment that includes intensive competition, product innovation and a rising scale of exposures to risks;

(b)   Control risks: internal supervision and protection mechanisms tend to reduce control risks in banks. Deregulation has loosened supervision in certain areas, thus contributing to potential increases in control risks. The growth in the complexity of financial markets has accelerated the development of sophisticated real-time electronic data processing systems, which have greatly improved the potential for control, but have in turn brought with them additional risks arising from the possibility of computer failure or fraud;

(c)   Detection risks: the increasing complexity of banking activities and the continuing development of new products and banking practices challenge the auditor's knowledge and understanding of banks' businesses and their associated risks. Expanding off balance sheet activities and complex financial instruments, which have not been matched by the concurrent development of internal controls, accounting principles and auditing practices, has left auditors exposed to a risk of inadequate professional support for their responsibilities.

The consistently changing regulatory environments force auditors to keep apprised of recent regulatory changes, and it may be argued that the auditing profession is unable to unilaterally work through existing regulatory and professional structures to make significant progress in meeting the developing needs of users of financial information.

In addition, in the last decade regulators have laid further responsibilities and duties on bank auditors. Increasingly, auditors are obligated to report to the supervisory authorities on certain matters, or else there is a tripartite agreement (or trilateral meetings) among the bank management, supervisory authorities and auditors requiring direct disclosures of certain matters to the authorities in specified circumstances.

In conclusion, the audit risks and responsibilities of banks' auditors have been dramatically increased in recent years and go far beyond those of auditors in other industries.

V. CONCLUSIONS AND FINAL RECOMMENDATIONS

A. The future of commercial banking

Banks everywhere are likely to experience a marked decline in their role in direct intermediation or asset transformation. Thus their traditional role of accepting deposits and extending short-term credit will continue to diminish. Instead, they will increase their involvement in indirect intermediation, specializing in and servicing capital markets. Also, economies of scale involving information will take on a major role. It can be expected that banks will expand activities whenever they can take advantage of joint production of information services, for example in credit card systems, trust activities and insurance. However, most developing countries lack efficient capital markets and will probably continue to rely heavily on financial intermediaries, especially banks, to maintain their traditional primary role in economic and monetary systems. Banks will usually be subject to restrictive regulation but will not necessarily be closely supervised.

The move to freer market mechanisms in developed countries is intimately connected with the move to deregulation and less government involvement in financial markets. The growing role of free-market determination of price and quantity in financial markets, together with the evolution of securitization and asset liquidation, has laid the foundations for market-based valuation in banks and similar financial institutions. Opposition to market-value accounting centres on the difficulty of making accurate market-value (fair-value) estimates of assets and liabilities. It is claimed that historical cost accounting has the important advantage of being easy to apply and is not subjective. In addition, it is considered inappropriate to apply market values to assets being held to maturity. Proponents of market-value accounting principles argue that only market-value accounting enables users of financial statements to have an indication of the economic net worth of a bank, as well as of its economic exposure to market risks and credit risks related to certain positions. The adoption of market-value accounting has the advantage of making a bank's financial condition more transparent.

Today it seems that the accounting profession is not ready to take the step of changing from the historically based valuation rules for all financial instruments. However, several countries and IASC have recently taken the approach of requiring disclosures about the fair value of financial instruments.

Another important accounting subject evolving from the changed environment of banks is the increasing demand for information about risk exposures and risk management of banks. Public disclosure will increase market efficiency and support market discipline. Banks should provide a meaningful description of the risks associated with their activities, particularly credit risks, concentration of credit risks, interest rate risks, market risks, liquidity risks and other operating risks resulting from on balance sheet or off balance sheet transactions, and a description of their ability to manage these risks. More public information about the risks incurred by banks will better enable users to evaluate and monitor them and may act as a deterrent to excessive risk-taking.

However, in the case of BCCI, more disclosure would not have helped depositors, but more transparency would have helped the regulators who are supposed to protect depositors. One problem in the BCCI case was cross-commitments between individuals and institutions. BCCI was really an issue of inadequate and non-transparent internal controls. Questions were also raised about what was and should be the role and responsibilities of the board of directors and the auditors of a multinational banking institution. Furthermore, there are no international laws or rules on liquidation of banks, and in the case of BCCI different groups affected by the collapse received compensation for varying proportions of the losses they sustained.

There are other important accounting issues concerning banks that need to be addressed by standard-setters, such as impairment of financial assets, loan restructurings, hedge accounting and derivative financial instruments, incorporating the time value of money into the accounts, and sale and transfer of assets. Rapid changes in financial markets and the development of new financial instruments have outstripped the accounting techniques used to measure profitability and risks. In the case of banks, these problems can adversely affect the reliability of regulatory reports necessary for prudential supervision.

The lack of international standardization in the above-mentioned areas has distorted the comparability of the capital positions of international banks. But this issue has been taken up by various forums of regulators, such as the Basle Committee. Their initiatives reflect the way in which the development of global markets has increased the need for international coordination of regulatory policies and convergence in their content.

B. Towards improved bank disclosures

IASC in its project on comparability and the European Union through its Council directives have created a framework that will eliminate the lack of uniformity that is currently permitted in the rules and requirements imposed in different countries. However, IASC does not provide a full set of disclosure rules, and the Council directives apply only to member countries and are therefore adapted exclusively to the European economic environment.

This chapter has presented recommendations for broader disclosures for banking enterprises operating in either a domestic or an international environment. It endeavours to broaden the scope of traditional bank disclosures, particularly for standard-setters in developing countries and countries in transition. On the one hand, the establishment of a universal disclosure system requires a proposal for a broad structure that will be able to accommodate the differences arising from variations in the banking systems and money and capital markets throughout the world. On the other hand, due consideration must be given to the preservation of the benefits inherent in the information required under the specific disclosure rules of any particular country.

This consideration has led to the dispersal of the recommended information among the primary financial statements, the notes and other parts of the annual report. One of the outcomes is therefore that in certain countries the details of the main reports may be broader than the proposed format of this chapter, but in other countries there is a possibility that a substantial part of the secondary details in the notes are superfluous. A possible solution to this problem in accordance with the guidance in this chapter is to permit flexibility in the choice of level of detail or grouping, subject to the principle of substantiality which will be determined by an enterprise's management. The degrees of freedom in this choice, as in the matter of possible derogation from the proposed disclosure rules, should be a function of the overriding principle requiring proper disclosure of the financial condition and business results of operations.

The importance attached to this last problem derives from the belief that unsuitable information, which is insufficient or excessive information, is detrimental to the effectiveness of the information contained in the reports and may even render it ineffective altogether. In other words, in parallel with the concern for full disclosure, care must be exercised to ensure that the reports are not unnecessarily cumbersome. True and fair disclosure in each of the parts of the annual report will provide users with the necessary information to evaluate the bank and the results of its activities, and facilitate the making of informed decisions.

Notes

1   Section 720 of the International Federation of Accountants' International Standards on Auditing, requires an auditor to read the information accompanying the financial statements in order to determine whether any material inconsistencies are contained therein. If that proves to be the case, the auditor should require that such information be amended. Many countries have similar standards.

2   When balances with the government are substantial they should be presented separately.

3   See footnote 2.

4   IASC, IAS 32, Financial Instruments: Disclosure and Presentation, para. 19.

5   Ibid., para. 58.

6   United States Securities and Exchange Commission (SEC) Regulation S-K requires the disclosure of forward-looking information. FRR 36 (SEC Financial Regulation Release No. 36, 1989) differentiates between prospective information, for which disclosure is required, and forecasts, for which disclosure is optional.

7   Para. 5(1) of Schedule 9 of the Company Law.

8   IAS 32, paras. 33-34.

9   Ibid., para. 36.

10 The manner in which the British Banking Association SORP relates to netting does not prevent netting from being followed in a situation in which more than two parties are involved, such as the

case of a mutual guarantee which creates the right of netting between the accounts of related companies on condition that "the relationship is in substance a single banking relationship". Even though the guideline in the British SORP appears to be broader, the IASC requirement for an agreement between the parties is a practical one (see IAS 32, paras. 36 and 41).

[11]   IAS 30, para. 13.

[12]   Council Directive of 8 December 1986 on the Annual Accounts and Consolidated Accounts of Banks and Other Financial Institutions (86/635/EEC), Article 23.

Bibliography

American Institute of Certified Public Accountants (AICPA).   Industry Audit Guide: Audits of Banks. New York, 1994.

Basle Committee on Banking Supervision and the Technical Committee of the International Organization of Securities Commissions (IOSCO). Framework for supervisory information about the derivatives activities of banks and securities firms. Basle, May 1995.

Basle Committee on Banking Supervision and the Technical Committee of the International Organization of Securities Commissions (IOSCO). Public disclosure of the trading and derivatives activities of banks and securities firms. Basle, November 1995.

British Banking Association (BBA). *Accounting Guide*. Basle, 1994.

British Banking Association. Statements of Recommended Practice (SORP) (mainly SORP on securities, and SORP on advances).

European Council Directives 86/635/EEC, 77/780/EECC and 78/660/EEC.

IAS 30, Disclosures in the Financial Statements of Banks and Similar Financial Institutions; IAS 32, Financial Instruments: Disclosure and Presentation.

Swary, I. and B. Topf. *Global Financial Deregulation: Commercial Banks at the Crossroads*. London, Basil Blackwell, 1992.

United Kingdom. Companies Act 1985 (Bank Accounts), Regulations 1991.

United Kingdom. Accounting Standards Committee (ASC). Statements of Standard Accounting Practice (SSAP).

United Kingdom. Accounting Standards Board (ASB). Financial Reporting Standards (FRS).

United States. Securities and Exchange Commission (SEC). Regulation S-X, Regulation S-K and industry guides.

United States. SEC. Financial Regulatory Release (FRR).

United States. SEC. Staff Accounting Bulletins (SAB).

United States. Financial Accounting Standards Board (FASB) pronouncements: Statement of Financial Accounting Standards (SFAS), FASB Concepts and FASB Interpretations.

United States. FASB. Prospectus on Disclosure Effectiveness. November 1995.

Woods, R. and M. Lafferty. *Bank Annual Reports: 1992 World Survey*.

CHAPTER III

ACCOUNTING FOR GOVERNMENT CONCESSIONS AND OTHER BENEFITS[1]

SUMMARY AND CONCLUSIONS

At its fourteenth session, ISAR considered the report entitled "Accounting and reporting for government concessions". A report on a related subject - "Accounting for government grants" (E/C.10/AC.3/1994/6) - had been considered at its twelfth session, in 1994, and the conclusion was reached that accounting for concessions deserved further and more detailed attention. Subsequently, the report on government concessions was prepared. It covered accounting for various types of government concessions: services contracts; build/operate/transfer (BOT) transactions; concessions for the use or operation of public assets; management contracts; and various other privileges or advantages given by governments to enterprises. The principles contained in this chapter could be useful to international and national standard-setters in the formulation of accounting standards. IAS 20, Accounting for Government Grants and Disclosure of Government Assistance, deals with the economic benefits provided by governments (assistance) and the transfer of resources (grants) to an enterprise. However, this standard does not apply to benefits which are provided indirectly, such as the provision of infrastructure in development areas or forms of assistance which cannot reasonably be valued. Government concessions, as defined in this chapter, are not specifically dealt with by IAS 20; however, the principles developed in IAS 20 and in this chapter are consistent.

During the discussion, the representative of **Morocco** said that, in some situations, the transferor might also grant monopolistic rights as part of a concession agreement. Since a grantee's cost in respect of services rendered or to be rendered affected charges to consumers, a concession holder had special fiduciary responsibilities to justify the reported costs so that regulators could adequately protect consumers.

The representative of **Germany** made the point that although, from an economic standpoint, certain concessions might grant the use of assets for a period equalling or exceeding their useful life, as in the situation that occurred for so-called financial leases, the laws of a country should not allow the capitalization of the cost of use. In the case of so-called economic ownership, the most suitable solution might be the capitalization of the asset in the accounts of the grantee, not of the owner, provided that the right of use (of the grantee) was legally enforced.

The representative of **Brazil** felt that the document before the Group was an important paper because very little accounting guidance had been published in the area in question and most countries in the process of privatization had to deal with many of the transactions concerned.

Several delegations expressed the belief that tax benefits and import and export concessions granted by a government should not be disclosed in general-purpose financial statements and that the topic should be more appropriately addressed in a study on tax reporting. The relevant paragraphs have been deleted from this chapter.

The Group concluded that UNCTAD should publish the report, which follows. Furthermore, the International Accounting Standards Committee's consideration and response would be solicited.

INTRODUCTION

This chapter is intended to give guidance on accounting and reporting issues relating to concessions received from governments, because at the present time there is no comprehensive international standard in this area. In some developing countries and countries in transition, concessions are very significant and widely used to attract foreign direct investment and technology. They may be used even more intensively in the future because the arrangements allow governments to shift the provision of public services to the private sector, thus enabling them to concentrate on activities which have greater priority and/or which are non-transferable. Hence, there is a growing demand for addressing this topic.

Concessions can be, and frequently are, granted by national, regional (state) or municipal governments (herein called the grantor) to an enterprise (referred to as the grantee or concessionaire), which may be publicly held or privately owned or could be quasi-governmental, to operate a public service, carry out public works or make use of public assets. Such concessions are usually for a fixed and possibly long-term period during which the enterprise provides the management and other personnel and assumes certain operating risks.

Concession contracts are divided into three common basic types, as follows:

(a)   service contracts (also called contracting-out transactions and concessions of public services);

(b)   build/operate/transfer transactions (also called concessions of public works); and

(c)   concessions to use and/or operate public assets.

Usually, the concession of the right to operate a public service, carry out a public works project or make use of public assets is made through a tender offering by the grantor in which each applicant presents a proposal comprising the terms of the contract, the estimated capital and operating costs, the compensation price and the means of payment, among other details. In this manner, the successful applicant will then undertake the activity in accordance with the terms and conditions which the grantor proposes.

The following paragraphs describe the characteristics of each of the above three types of concession contracts and the accounting treatment for transactions under the various arrangements. Other types of transactions between governments and enterprises which are not exactly government concessions but which should be treated as such are also considered in this chapter.

I. GENERAL CONCEPTS

Revenues and costs incurred in connection with concession agreements should normally be accounted for on an accrual basis. Before a concession contract is issued by a government body, any costs incurred by the prospective grantee, particularly in connection with obtaining the concession, should usually be recorded as expenses of the period in which they were incurred. However, such costs may be deferred if the prospective grantee has reasonable evidence that the concession will be granted and the costs are clearly and specifically associated with the potential project.

When the grantee has to pay for the right to be granted a concession, this payment would usually be in the form of a front-end fee. The payment, or the incurring of a liability to make a future payment, should be capitalized by the grantee as an intangible asset and amortized on a straight line basis over the life of the concession or according to a proportional method in relation to operating income if that would achieve a better matching of costs and revenues. If the transaction calls for the transfer of shares of the operating enterprise, or of another enterprise, as consideration for the value of the concession, the grantee should record the value of the concession obtained as an intangible asset subject to amortization with a corresponding credit in the appropriate stockholders' equity accounts for the fair value of the rights received or of the shares of stock, whichever is the more accurately estimatable.

II. SERVICE CONTRACTS

These types of arrangements are usually specified in a contract in which the government grants an enterprise the right to carry out a specific public service using its own management and incurring the operating risks for a fixed period of time. The enterprise is entitled to charge consumers for the services rendered at rates which include a profit margin. Service contracts may also provide for a specified sum of money to be paid by the grantee to the grantor. The grantee sometimes uses assets owned by the grantor, which are returnable at the end of the contract together with any additional assets which the grantee owns. Examples of such assets are buildings which are constructed on public land and used by the grantee during the period of the contract. Among the most common examples of public services operated by private sector and quasi-governmental enterprises through government concessions are gas, water, electric energy, telephone, public transport, garbage collection and public sanitation services.

A. Accounting treatment for rights to operate public services

The right to operate a public service may be granted either free or at a cost to the grantee. If the right is granted for a specified amount that is paid in advance, or for which there is an obligation to pay a defined fee at a later date, the cost of the right should be recorded as an intangible asset of the enterprise. This asset should then be amortized over the term of the contract on a straight line basis or according to some other rational method that matches the expense for the accounting period with the benefits derived from the agreement.

Another type of transaction could be for an amount equal to the accumulated amortization of the intangible asset (the cost of the rights) to be paid to the grantor at the conclusion of the concession instead of in advance. However, the timing of the payment should have no effect on when the expense is recorded in the accounts. If the cost is paid monthly, the payment should be charged to an expense account in the records of the enterprise unless there is a mismatching of the amount of the payment with the benefits received.

It is also conceivable that the consideration given to the government could be an equity interest in the grantee. This often occurs when a corporation is formed specifically for the purpose of being the recipient of a concession contract. In this situation the enterprise should record the fair value of the rights obtained as additions to its stockholders' equity accounts.

In other situations the concession rights might be granted at no cost. Regardless of whether there is a cost involved, the grantee should disclose the existence of the rights and the benefits to be derived therefrom in the notes to its financial statements, including details of the obligations which arise under the agreement.

B. Accounting for assets used in the operations of a concession

From an accounting point of view, one of the most controversial aspects of concessions occurs when assets owned by the grantor are transferred to the grantee for operating purposes. If the concession agreement calls for the grantee to pay the grantor for the assets, the following could occur:

(a)   The grantee could immediately pay cash for the assets or agree to make payments at a later date. In this case, the grantee should record the fixed assets and liabilities, if any, on the records of the operating enterprise;

(b)   The grantee could exchange shares of stock of the operating enterprise, or of another enterprise, as consideration for the value of the operating assets transferred by the government. In this case, the grantee should record the fixed assets and corresponding credits in the appropriate stockholders' equity accounts for the fair value of the assets received or of the shares of stock exchanged, whichever is the more accurately estimatable.

Another type of transaction might involve the government's transferring certain operating assets to the grantee for use in operations, with the ownership title to those assets being retained by the grantor. The assets essentially become the grantee's operating assets. They should continue to be recorded in the accounts of the owner (that is, the government) and no assets would be recorded by the grantee. However, if the grantee believes that the best disclosure from an economic disclosure viewpoint would be to record the cost of the use of the assets through periodic depreciation charges, an acceptable alternative would be for the grantee also to record the value of the assets on its books. Depreciation should be calculated in the same manner as for the grantee's other fixed assets or as a function of the term of the contract, whichever is shorter. Furthermore, a deferred revenue amount should also be recorded that is equal to the value of the assets, and this deferred credit would be amortized using the same method as used to depreciate the assets. This methodology could be used when:

(a)   Such assets generate income for the grantee and not for the grantor; and therefore the assets should be reflected on the books of the grantee. The government may receive income under the terms of the concession agreement in relationship to the depreciation expense. Therefore, keeping the assets in the accounts of the grantor does not reflect the economic substance of the concession agreement;

(b)   The grantee has control as well as use of the concession assets similar to a financial lease transaction; and therefore this control should be reflected in its records; and

(c)   Concession agreements are usually for a long duration and the assets might have no value to the grantor at the end of the concession period.

The grantee should disclose in the explanatory notes to the financial statements, in addition to the general disclosure items referred to previously, information on the assets utilized, their book value and their life expectancy. There also may be a provision for such assets to be returned to the grantor if the grantee becomes insolvent or under certain other contingent circumstances as specified in the concession contract. If this is the case, the information should also be disclosed.

A third type of transaction might be for assets to be transferred to the grantee free of charge. In this situation the fair value of the assets should be considered as a donation to the grantee and recorded as such. The general treatment for government donations is for the grantee to record the assets received at their fair value and also record a deferred income account which would be subsequently amortized as the asset is depreciated. However, in certain countries it is allowable to record donations in a special account in the shareholders' equity section bearing the title "Donated Surplus" or a similar one. A description of the accounting followed should be included in the footnotes to the financial statements.

C. Maintenance of returnable assets

In order to be able to return assets used in the operation of a concession to a condition that is acceptable to the grantor in accordance with the concession agreement, or in order to be able to achieve optimal utility from concession assets, the grantee may need currently or prospectively to renovate and/or repair the assets. Such renovations may require large expenditures for materials, parts, labour and other costs which would affect the financial results of the operating enterprise, especially if the assets are not operational for an extended period of time, which would prevent them from being used to generate revenues. The grantee should make current period provisions for significant costs for the renovation and/or repairs before undertaking such actions. The provisions would then be reduced by the amount of costs incurred when the renovation and repairs are effected. The purpose of this method is to match properly the revenues and expenses in an accounting period by distributing the costs of renovation and repairs over the entire period during which the assets are used. This will result in a more accurate measurement of the net income of each accounting period.

D. Accounting for concession assets at the termination of the concession agreement

If the grantee has title to enterprise operating assets, but they cannot be retained for its use in other activities, either because they must be returned to the grantor or because they have special uses or have no other commercial value to the grantee, the net book value of the assets should be written off in the grantee's accounting records. Property improvements to public land provided under a concession agreement fall into this category. If the grantee has estimated operating costs reasonably accurately, the net book value of the assets would be zero at this point in time because the book value should be equal to the residual value, which in this case is zero, and the asset should have been fully depreciated over the duration of the contract. Therefore, only in the event of miscalculation of the depreciation and amortization or an early cancellation of the concession contract would a net book value other than zero be expected.

If the grantee is to be paid for the assets returned to the grantor or transferred to another enterprise having a new concession for the operations, the amount could be a specified value, the fair value (which is more frequently the case) or the net book value of the assets. Any difference between the amount to be paid and the net book value of the assets to be transferred should be recorded as a gain or loss in the appropriate accounting period. Losses should be recorded in the accounting period when they are reasonably estimatable. However, gains should not be recorded until the accounting period when their realization is certain.

E. Fees payable by the grantee to the grantor as payment for supervision and other services

If the grantee is contractually obligated to make payments to the grantor for its services, such as for supervision, monitoring and control of the quality of the public services, such fees should be recorded as normal operating expenses of the concession enterprise when incurred.

III. BUILD/OPERATE/TRANSFER TRANSACTIONS

Build/operate/transfer transactions (commonly called BOT transactions) give the grantee the right to construct or buy and operate a certain public work. BOT transactions typically occur under a long-term contract to construct infrastructure projects such as roads, railways, bridges, viaducts, dams, airports and tunnels, which take several years to complete. These transactions are usually entered into as a means for the government to finance the construction of a public work. The grantee receives from the grantor the right to carry out the specific project and be suitably remunerated. In this case, the remuneration received normally comprises the payment for the construction costs incurred and a profit margin. Sometimes the grantee is entitled to operate the public works project after its completion in order to generate income. The operating income enables the grantee to recover the construction costs and the operating and maintenance expenses and to earn a profit margin. The grantee normally would also be allowed to recover any amounts that were paid to the government for the concession rights. At the end of the term of the concession the project assets and operating rights are transferred to the grantor.

A. Costs

Costs incurred for the construction of public works might include:

(a)   materials used in the construction of the project, depreciation of fixed assets used in the work, etc.;

(b)   labour costs related directly to the specific contract, i.e. costs of labour on the construction site, including supervision;

(c)   indirect costs such as insurance, technical assistance, and indirect construction expenses; and

(d)   general or overhead costs such as administrative expenses or financial costs.

B. Accounting for income earned from a concession

The operating revenues earned under a BOT contract should be recognized when it is possible to generate income through the provision of services, usually to third parties, and when the related costs and expenses have been incurred or can be estimated. Otherwise, payments received from governments and others should be deferred as liabilities (deferred or unearned income) and revenues should not be accrued into the profit and loss accounts for the accounting period.

When the grantee has the right to receive income from the operation of a public work after its construction, the construction costs incurred should be charged to fixed assets accounts - for example, in the case of road construction, where the income is generated from the right to collect tolls. In one of the largest BOT transactions in history, the grantees who are responsible for the construction of the tunnel which links the United Kingdom and France have until the year 2041 to recover their investment through operations before they have to turn the operations back to the grantors of the operating rights.

Income for the construction of a public work should be recognized using the "percentage of completion" method of accounting for construction projects if the amounts earned can be reasonably accurately estimated during the period of construction. As an alternative, if the amounts earned cannot be estimated reasonably accurately the grantee may use the "completed contract" method of accounting, which would mean that construction earnings would be recognized upon the conclusion of the construction phase of the contract when the work has been completed to the satisfaction of the government. These two methods of accounting are accrual methods, which mean that the recording of income would be made when earned according to the principles described in this paragraph regardless of when amounts become billable to the government for cash flow purposes - either on an interim basis or on completion of the project.

To achieve a proper matching of costs incurred and revenues earned, all pre-construction and construction costs should be capitalized when incurred (i.e. paid or an obligation incurred to make payments at a later date) into asset accounts in the records of the grantee. Such amounts would then be transferred to accounting period profit and loss accounts when the related income is earned on the accrual basis. If this method of accounting is not followed, the profit and loss accounts in the years of concession operations might show only the expenses incurred, and thus losses; and the year in which revenues are received in cash would show the earnings, which might not have been earned exclusively in that year. Of course, if all the construction is completed and the revenues are earned in the same accounting period, there would be no violation of the generally accepted concept of the matching principle of accounting.

In applying the "percentage of completion" method of construction accounting, the revenues earned during accounting periods may be estimated on the basis of the:

(a)   costs incurred during the year as a percentage of the total estimated costs of the project; or

(b)   revenue recognized on the basis of a technical report on the extent of the project's completion.

The percentage of the proportion of completion in method (b) should be applied to the amount of the total revenue set forth in the concession agreement. Also, related pre-construction and construction period costs should be charged to the same accounting period's profit and loss accounts, whether or not such costs have been actually paid in cash. However, for large and complex public works, particularly those with sub-projects of variable durations, it may be difficult to use one single percentage of completion with respect to the entire project. In this situation the ratio of costs incurred over the year to the total costs of the works is the best method to be applied to the total agreed revenues for the construction phase.

The use of either of these two methods permits the income to be distributed among the periods in which the work is performed, or the costs are incurred, and results in a more accurate economic measurement over time of net income for each year or interim accounting period than does recognizing all of the revenues and costs and expenses at the completion of the contract.

C. Accounting for advance payments

Cash advances received for services to be performed in the future should be recorded as liabilities since the payments represent an obligation by an enterprise to perform services at a later date. If for some reason this is not possible, the advances would have to be returned under normal circumstances. Advances received which exceed the income earned in the period should remain under the "liabilities" section of the accounts until the services are rendered or the advance payments have been returned.

D. Provision for losses

When a loss is incurred under a contract, whether from construction or from operation of the project, it should be immediately recognized by the grantee as an expense in the current accounting period.

E. Transfer of the public works assets to the grantor following the termination of the concession agreement

When the agreement states that the grantee should not be fully or partially reimbursed for the assets transferred to the government at the end of the contract period, the grantee's compensation is the revenues from the operation of the concession. In this case the assets should be depreciated down to their net realizable value, if any, at the conclusion of the contract. Generally, the net book value upon disposal will be equal to the amount of the repayment, since the rate of depreciation must take into account the residual value of the concession assets. Any difference from what was recorded would be recognized as a gain or loss from the revision of an estimate in the accounting period when determinable. If the contract states that the asset should be transferred at fair value, any difference between that amount and the net book value is recorded in the profit and loss account.

F. Disclosures

In addition to the appropriate disclosures referred to in previous paragraphs of this chapter, the notes to the financial statements of concessions for the construction of public works should include the total value of the assets, the stage of completion at the balance sheet date, and the method adopted to recognize revenues.

IV. CONCESSIONS FOR THE USE OR OPERATION OF PUBLIC ASSETS

A concession to use and/or operate public property assets (usually fixed assets) is normally for a specified purpose and period of time. The grantee may compensate the grantor for the use of the assets. The grantee normally has temporary possession of the property and should be liable for all the costs and expenses and risks of using the assets or operating the activity to which the concession relates. Concessions to use buildings near public roads, such as service stations, restaurants and snack-bars, are examples of this type of arrangement.

Because ownership of the assets remains with the grantor, they should continue to be recorded on the books of the grantor as fixed assets together with the corresponding depreciation charges. A concession for the use of the assets is similar to an operating lease contract which specifies that recording fixed assets in the accounts of the grantor is an appropriate accounting treatment. However, it may be that the term of the concession is equal to or in excess of the economic and/or physical lives of the assets, in which case the grantee might record the assets and related depreciation expenses as if the transaction were being accounted for as a financing lease.

If the grantee makes improvements to the concession assets which are not subject to reimbursement from the grantor and which result in a longer life expectancy for the assets, the expenditures should be recorded as "improvements to third parties' property" and be reported with other fixed asset accounts. Such amounts should be amortized over the remaining term of the concession contract or the life of the assets, whichever is shorter.

If the concession agreement requires periodic payments for the use of the assets, such payments should be recorded appropriately and proportionately as operating expenses in the period in a manner which matches the costs with the benefits (revenues) obtained from the operation of the concession. If the payment is made in full at the beginning of the contract, it should be reported as a fixed asset or prepaid expense and amortized over the period of the concession. If the grantee has recorded the assets as if under a financing lease, the offsetting liability would be periodically reduced by the payments made to the grantor of the concession. If the use of the assets is free of charge, the grantee would only disclose the benefit in the notes to the financial statement of the enterprise.

Usually, grantees are contractually liable for returning to the government in good condition the public property that they have been using, taking into consideration normal wear and tear. Hence the grantee must routinely repair and maintain buildings and other long-lived assets. The grantee should make provisions during current operating periods for any large-scale expenditures for repairs and maintenance that are expected to be required at some future date.

In line with the disclosures referred to in the previous section of this chapter, the terms of the agreement, the characteristics of the property or other assets, the duration of the contract, the remaining term, the obligations of the grantee and any restrictions on the use of the assets should be disclosed.

V. MANAGEMENT CONTRACTS

Under a management contract a grantor such as a government assigns the operation of a commercial activity to a grantee, usually referred to as the "manager" of the activity. The purpose of a management contract is to obtain a party to operate a public service on behalf of the government; the latter, however, is still considered to be providing the service.

The grantor is usually responsible for all the expenses required for the operation of an activity, including the acquisition of materials and other appropriate assets and any operating and non-operating costs. The function of the manager is to execute the project through scheduling, supervising, consulting, and controlling the works or technical services.

A. Revenues for services performed

Many concession contracts have a term that lasts a number of years and in some situations the compensation (fees) may be fixed at the outset, or may be earned in relation to the costs incurred (commonly called a "cost plus" contract). The fees may be stated in the agreement as a fixed amount or may be a percentage of the costs incurred. If the income is received as a lump sum, it should be taken into the current period's profit and loss account, as in the case of long-term construction contracts, namely:

    (a)   using the percentage-of-completion accounting method;

    (b)   as a percentage of the costs incurred; or

    (c)   after all the contractual obligations have been performed.

As explained in an earlier section of this chapter, the first and second methods are preferred.

If the remuneration is on a cost plus basis, the accounting method is simplified since the revenues correlate directly to the costs incurred on an accrual basis.

B. Disclosures

The manager should disclose in explanatory footnotes to the financial statements the existence of the management contract and its terms and obligations, including the total value of the contracted revenue and the method used to account for it.

VI. OTHER PRIVILEGES AND BENEFITS GRANTED BY GOVERNMENTS

This section considers various privileges and benefits which may be granted by governments. The accounting treatments and disclosures, where different from the items described above, are briefly described. The listing of items below is not exhaustive; other benefits include monopoly rights, guaranteed rates or tariffs, and guaranteed minimum income or returns.

A. Licences for engaging in certain forms of economic activities

A licence is an authorization to carry out an economic activity. It is different from a concession, which is related to assets and services to be used for public purposes. A licence is a means by which a government can control the initiation and operation of an economic activity while providing for the security, health, safety and environmental protection of the citizenry. The licensee should disclose in the explanatory footnotes to the financial statements the term of the licence granted, the conditions to be complied with, and any possible difficulties that it may have or has had in meeting these conditions, and the resultant consequences.

B. Licences for manufacturing and distributing products in certain geographical areas

The granting of a licence by itself does not create special accounting and reporting implications. Expenses are usually incurred on a periodic basis for such licences and are typically relatively low and do not justify deferral as assets.

C. Agreements without tender offers

There are situations in which the government may purchase assets or hire services without tenders because the value of the transaction is insignificant; it is an emergency purchase; there is a particularly well recognized level of specialization by a certain supplier; or there is a monopoly for the goods or services to be provided. For the enterprise selected the transaction represents a normal commercial transaction. If any discount or special pricing arrangements are provided, the benefit given to the government should be accounted for as a reduction of normal gross revenues in the profit and loss accounts of the period. If the transaction is significant to the enterprise, it should be appropriately disclosed in the notes to the financial statements.

D. Rights to extract natural resources

Receipt of the right to extract natural resources is sometimes preceded by feasibility studies. The studies usually estimate the volume of the resources that exist, the quantity to be extracted, the amount of the revenues expected from exploiting the resources, and the costs necessary for executing the project. All the costs connected with investigating and securing the project should be charged to current profits and losses when incurred, or when there is a high probability of success, the costs and expenses for the pre-extraction phase can be deferred for matching with the sales revenues obtained in later accounting periods. In the absence of this probability, the enterprise should charge all such expenses to the profit and loss accounts of the period in which they were incurred.

If a project becomes operational, the enterprise should report periodically the costs which have been capitalized in order to begin the removal process. The percentage of depletion of the costs incurred in connection with the project is normally based on the volume of the current accounting period's production in relation to the estimated total reserves of the resources as of the beginning of the period. As an alternative accounting method this percentage may be expressed as a function of the period during which the licence holder has the right to exploit the resources. If the government receives in kind a portion of the production of the resources, any costs incurred by the enterprise related to the extraction or production of the government's share should be charged to the enterprise's profit and loss account for the period.

The enterprise should disclose in explanatory footnotes the size and stage of development of the project as well as the volume of the reserve of remaining resources in accordance with the latest survey, as reduced by subsequent quantities produced, removed or extracted from the properties.

E. Rights to acquire raw and other materials and services at preferential rates

This is another form of indirect government assistance. No special accounting treatment is required to record the benefits obtained unless costs are incurred. The enterprise should disclose in explanatory footnotes the existence and nature of the benefits, the duration of the agreement and the significance of the benefits as regards the financial results of the accounting period.

F. Leasing transactions including land, buildings and equipment

Leases between the government and a private enterprise normally represent an operating right for a public asset. Therefore, the lessee of the asset should record the rental expenses in the period's income statement. The enterprise should disclose in the notes to the financial statements the existence of the lease, the assets involved, their value and the resulting financial obligations and duration of the contract. If it is appropriate the lease could also be treated as a finance lease.

G. Rights to operate services such as a television network and radio stations

The rights to operate public services such as television and radio stations are often cancellable by the government if the enterprise does not follow certain specific operating rules. The cost of the rights may be charged to the profit and loss account or be capitalized as assets, if significant, in the accounting period in which the costs are incurred. All the other costs usually relate to the services rendered and they therefore constitute operational costs of the period concerned. All the costs of the property and equipment necessary for operating enterprises of this nature are capitalized and depreciated in the same way as for other operations. If the government charges a periodic fee for the licence, this amount should be charged to the profit and loss account for that period. The enterprise that holds the operating rights should disclose the kind of service for which it was granted the licence and its duration.

Note

[1] This Chapter was prepared with the assistance of Professor Lazaro Placido Lisboa, University of São Paulo, Brazil.

Bibliography

American Institute of Certified Public Accountants (AICPA). AICPA Professional Standards. Chicago, Commerce Clearing House Inc., 1991.

Conseil National de la Comptabilité (CNC). Rapport sur les Orientations en Matière de Comptabilité des Entreprises Concessionnaires. Paris, Imprimerie Nationale, 1994.

Financial Accounting Standards Board (FASB). Accounting Standards. Homewood, Illinois, Irwin, 1992/93.

Fundação Instituto de Pesquisas Contábeis Atuariais e Financeiras (FIPECAFI) and Arthur Andersen. *Normas e Prácticas Contábeis do Brasil*. São Paulo, Atlas, 1994.

Hendriksen, S. Eldon and M.S. Van Breda. *Accounting Theory*. Homewood, Illinois, Irwin, 1992.

Indícibus, S. de. *Teoria da Contabilidade*. São Paulo, Atlas, 1994.

Indícibus, S. de, E. Maratins and E. R. Gelbcke. *Manual de Contabilidade das Sociedades por Ações*, (FIPECAFI). São Paulo, Atlas, 1995.

Meirelles, H. Lopes. *Direito Administrativo Brasileiro*. Malheiros Editores, 1992

CHAPTER IV

COMPLIANCE WITH INTERNATIONAL ACCOUNTING STANDARDS[1]

SUMMARY AND CONCLUSIONS

At its fourteenth session ISAR considered a report titled "Compliance with international accounting standards" (TD/B/ITNC/AC.1/(XIV)/CRP.1). In the last five years there have been at least four major forces which have improved compliance:

(a)   a project by the International Accounting Standards Committee (IASC) to reduce the number of options contained in its standards and make them more comprehensive;

(b)   an investigation by the European Commission of the possibility of allowing member countries to prepare their consolidated accounts on the basis of international standards as promulgated by IASC;

(c)   use of national and international standards by some transnational corporations in an effort to raise funds in various capital markets;

(d)   an agreement between IASC and the International Organization of Securities Commissions (IOSCO) that once IASC produces a core set of standards which are acceptable to IOSCO, these will be recommended for use on all capital markets. This will be the single most compelling force for the further use of international accounting standards (IASs).

Efforts to harmonize international accounting can be classified into two main types: governmental efforts, as seen for example in ISAR, and the European Union; and private sector efforts, for example the work of IASC. Governmental efforts tend to be slow because of the lack of an explicit framework and the need for political compromise, and because national laws are difficult to alter. Private sector efforts, on the other hand, often have no legal authority, which means that the acceptance of the standards depends mostly on their usefulness.

This chapter investigates the obstacles to the acceptance of IASs. There is no doubt that great differences in national accounting exist. These are illustrated by the famous example of Daimler-Benz, which in 1993 reported a profit of over DM 600 million under German rules and a loss of over DM 1,800 million under United States rules. The following year these results were reversed.

Three of the main causes of national accounting differences and the related obstacles to harmonization are:

(a) unique historical events;

(b) external influences; and

(c) the differing purposes of financial statements for various users.

The **Chairperson** of the fourteenth session commented on the distinction made in the document between credit-based countries and equity market countries and the differences this caused in their accounting standards. He thought that the participation of the private sector in standard-setting in the equity market countries was preferable to the situation that prevailed in the credit-based countries, where rule-making was in the hands of governments. He wondered whether the Group could assist governments in moving to more self-regulation and amending legislation to bring it into line with IASs. He hoped that, in the future, TNCs wishing to seek listings on foreign security exchanges would not need to prepare multiple sets of financial statements, but one set based on international accounting standards. Harmonized standards were also needed for non-global players such as small and medium-sized enterprises (SMEs).

Furthermore, he suggested that since ISAR was the only body where experts worked in the interests of government, it could present the views of governments to IASC for the development of international accounting standards. The representative of **IASC** thought that there was merit to this suggestion. Both the EU and IOSCO had observer status on the IASC Board. He informed the Group that IASC was moving rapidly towards producing a core set of standards acceptable to IOSCO by early 1998. IASC was also considering ways to help with the interpretation of its standards and in the future would be open to questions on their meaning and application. It remained as interested as ever in developing countries and countries in transition. It had undertaken a project on accounting for agriculture with funds from the World Bank.

A number of representatives, including those of **Brazil**, **Chile**, **China**, the **Republic of Korea**, **Poland**, **Thailand** and **Turkey**, made comments on and corrections to the information contained in document TD/B/ITNC/AC.1(XIV)/CRP.1, which were taken into account in the following chapter. Rapid progress in the development of capital markets in developing countries and the move of economies in transition to market economies made the precise classification of countries difficult. Thus, the situation in some countries had changed since early 1995 when the survey had been undertaken. Many countries felt that even though their accounting standards did not comply completely with international standards, sufficient progress had been made in this area and they would be better described as being "in partial compliance". The representative of the **Democratic Republic of the Congo** said that although his country was aware of IASs, it found them difficult to apply. There were problems with interpretation and also with the regulatory system, which embedded accounting rules in law and made them difficult to change in line with IASs. The representative of **Hungary** said that where accounting rules were legislated, the process involved was a very long one. His country had successfully implemented the EU directives and now companies were complying with IASs voluntarily. The representative of **Chile** stated that his country still followed accounting developments in the developed equity market countries, especially United States accounting standards (FAS), although IASs were increasingly accepted and used on the market and provided important guidelines when local standards were lacking in certain areas. The representative of **Sudan** said that in Sudan the work of ISAR and IASC was modified by local laws. A number of delegations felt that the use of IASs by enterprises would attract foreign direct investment and credit financing. The representative of **Nigeria** said that the report could be a useful tool in analysing the status of accounting within the African region. The representative of the **International Confederation of Free Trade Unions** stated that the report showed the obstacles to compliance and what steps needed to be taken. She added that banks were requiring the use of IASs even for non-global companies. She supported the idea of fuller participation by **IASC** in ISAR sessions, as did a number of other delegations.

The representative of **Morocco** suggested that it must be asked whether IASs were too sophisticated and costly for small and medium-sized enterprises to apply. Such enterprises might need simplified systems. The representative of of the **Democratic Republic of the Congo** said awareness of IASs was one matter, but their application was another. His country's accounting system was influenced by the French *plan comptable* and it was hard to integrate IASs into that system. This view was also expressed by the **Chairperson** and the representatives of **Denmark**, **France** and the **European Commission**. The European Commission had adopted a new accounting strategy under which it would enhance collaboration within Europe and avoid proposing new legislation as far as possible. Also, it encouraged the joint work of IOSCO and IASC for consolidated accounts of companies seeking listing on stock exchanges worldwide. The Contact Committee on the Accounting Directives had examined the conformity of IASs with EC directives, and found there were no major conflicts. The EC representative stressed that IASs were for listed companies' consolidated accounts. For individual company accounts, there was a long way to go to arrive at a common international language. The costs and benefits of having one uniform system must always be taken into account.

The observer from the **Canadian Institute of Chartered Accountants** questioned this viewpoint, since different rules for large and small companies would make a true and fair view difficult. Of course, small companies should not have to provide the detail that large companies provided, but this was a decision to be made at the national level. Inevitably, small companies grew larger, and it would be impractical if the accounting rules changed when they achieved a certain critical size. The representative of **Tunisia** held a similar view. He said that the accounting principles embodied within IASs were similar to the accounting principles of codified law countries and that these principles should not compromise the quantitative and qualitative characteristics of financial information. Furthermore, very few if any countries had accounting rules which were identical to the prescribed taxation treatment for certain items of income and expenditure.

The **Chairperson** said he was impressed that so many delegations had stressed the continuing need for ISAR to support further harmonization on a worldwide basis in the interests of all concerned. The lack of adequate accounting and auditing standards had been seen as a major obstacle for developing countries and countries in transition in their quest for growth, development and membership of the global economy. Harmonization of standards for cross-border listings would also create the need for a similar harmonization of standards for other enterprises (i.e. non-listed enterprises, and small and medium-sized enterprises), especially in developing countries and countries in transition.

Conclusions of the Group on compliance with IASs

The Group concluded that the text of document TD/B/ITNC/AC.1(XIV)/CRP.1 should be updated on the basis of the comments made in the Group, and then published.

It was evident that self-regulation was preferable, but it was not practised in all countries. There was a continuing need for further harmonization on a worldwide basis, taking into account the different objectives of users of financial statements. The lack of adequate accounting and auditing standards was a major obstacle for developing countries and countries in transition in their quest for growth, development and integration into the global economy. The codified law countries preferring credit-based accounting standards should consider how they could improve participation in standard-setting in their countries. Harmonization of standards for cross-border listings might also create the need for the harmonization of standards for other enterprises (i.e. non-listed enterprises, and small and medium-sized enterprises), especially in developing countries and countries in transition.

The Group proposed that:

(a)   existing IASs be reviewed to determine whether they were consistent with the interests of all enterprises; such a review should take into account the cost/benefit ratio of accounting and auditing, the question of the size of enterprises, and the need to maintain business confidentiality in sensitive areas in order not to jeopardize competitive positions;

(b)   cooperation with other international organizations involved in standard-setting should be further improved in order to enhance the formulation and utilization of international accounting standards.

INTRODUCTION

The purpose of the present review is different from the purpose of those undertaken in the past in that ISAR wanted to focus this time on the reasons for non-compliance.[2] In the past the financial statements of transnational corporations had been examined to determine the degree of *de facto* compliance with ISAR's Conclusions on Accounting and Reporting by *Transnational Corporations*.[3] In a 1990 survey, the financial statements of 194 enterprises were analysed with regard to 39 accounting items. The overall score for disclosure was 59 per cent. The main conclusion of the survey was that harmonization efforts must be accompanied by periodic monitoring and more effective mechanisms to ensure compliance.

During the last five years a number of efforts have been undertaken to improve compliance. ISAR's mandate was renewed in 1991. At that time it was recommended that ISAR contribute to national, regional and international standard-setting by focusing on technical cooperation, particularly to meet the needs of developing countries and countries in transition in the development of the accounting profession and standard-setting. At the same time other international groups such as the International Accounting Standards Committee (IASC) began an effort to reduce the number of options contained in its International Accounting Standards (IASs) and make them more comprehensive in the hope that they would be more acceptable to global organizations such the International Organization of Securities Commissions (IOSCO). The European Commission was investigating ways of allowing corporations in member countries to prepare their consolidated accounts on the basis of international accounting standards. Some transnational corporations have begun to comply on a voluntary basis both with the IASs and with their national standards in order to provide the financial information required for raising funds in various international capital markets.

While the mandate of ISAR is to review standard-setting at the national, regional and international levels and to promote harmonization, it is the mandate of IASC to actually formulate and promote international standards. Since this chapter seeks to identify the chief obstacles which prevent countries from complying on a *de jure* or *de facto* basis with international standards, it was decided to make that evaluation on the basis of the IASs.

I. INTERNATIONAL ACCOUNTING STANDARDS

The International Accounting Standards Committee was founded in 1973 by professional accountancy bodies from nine countries. Currently, 114 such bodies from 85 countries are members. IASC's objectives are:

(a)   to formulate and publish in the public interest accounting standards to be observed in the presentation of financial statements and to promote their worldwide acceptance and observance; and

(b)   to work generally for the improvement and harmonization of regulations, accounting standards and procedures relating to the presentation of financial statements.

IASC's work is controlled by its Board, which is currently composed of representatives of 13 countries[4] and three co-opted bodies. A two-thirds majority of the Board is required for issuing an exposure draft, and a three-quarters majority for issuing a standard. The Board has a consultative group, including representatives from ISAR, the European Commission and IOSCO. Although IASC is independent of other bodies, it has a relationship with the International Federation of Accountants (IFAC) whereby the members of the two bodies are identical and IFAC funds part of the work of IASC.

International accounting harmonization efforts can be characterized as falling into two main types:

Model A - governmental. Such a process involves government representatives (civil servants, particularly lawyers) in preparing draft laws without an explicit conceptual framework. The process is slow and the laws are difficult to alter. Because of the need for political compromise, many issues are left out or covered by national options. Nevertheless, enforceable laws result. The work of the European Union in adopting company law directives to harmonize accounting falls into this category.

Model B - private sector. Such a process involves accounting experts in drafting international standards which have no legal authority. Given that standards are not binding, that governments are not represented and that unanimity is not required, it is possible eventually to cover all significant issues and to minimize the available options. The status and authority of the standards depend on the respectability of the due process and the conceptual framework of the standard-setters, and on whether the standards are useful. IASC's work falls into this type.

Philosophically, model A harmonization is associated with codified law countries (such as Germany, Italy and Japan), where the government controls accounting and where the collection of tax, the protection of creditors and the calculation of legal levels of dividends are major uses for accounting. Model B harmonization is associated with common law countries (such as the United States of America, the United Kingdom and Australia), where accounting rules are traditionally made by accountants and where the prime objective of financial reporting is to provide information to users for making financial decisions.

Recently, several developments have raised IASC's status:

(a)   A conceptual framework was issued in 1989;

(b)   A project to improve IASs was begun in 1989 and led to the issue of ten revised standards in 1993;

(c)   In 1993, IOSCO accepted IAS 7 (cash flow accounting) for cross-border financial reporting purposes, and in 1995 it agreed to IASC's four-year work plan designed to lead to acceptance of all core standards;

(d)   Certain jurisdictions (e.g. Hong Kong in 1993)[5] and several companies (e.g. Bayer AG in Germany in 1994)[6] have adopted IASs as a basis for financial reporting; and

(e)   The staffing, funding and publication output of IASC have increased. By the end of 1995, IASC had issued 32 standards, of which two had been replaced and one was non-mandatory.[7]

II. THE CAUSES OF DIFFERENCE AND THE RELATED OBSTACLES TO HARMONIZATION

This section takes for granted that there are great differences in national accounting practices and that this is a problem which should be addressed. Perhaps the most famous example of the differences was the adjustment of Daimler-Benz's 1993 earnings from a profit of DM 615 million under German rules to a loss of DM 1,839 million under United States rules. (The 1994 adjustment was in the opposite direction, increasing profit from DM 895 million to DM 1,052 million.) The sheer scale of these differences, and the fact that many accounting areas contribute to them, illustrate the magnitude of the obstacle to harmonization.

This section examines three of the main causes of national differences, and the related obstacles to harmonization. It is suggested that some differences are caused by unique events, some by forces external to a country and some by different purposes as regards financial reporting.

A. Unique events

In many cases, the differences may result from unique historical events. For example, the three most obvious differences between practices in the United States and the United Kingdom might be characterized in that way:

(a)   Last-in, first-out inventory valuation (LIFO). The United States tax authorities were reluctant to allow the use of LIFO in the 1930s; therefore, they accepted it for tax purposes, but only if companies were also using it for accounting purposes. This is consistent with the normal procedure whereby tax authorities generally follow accounting practices. However, it has naturally led to an accounting choice of LIFO by many companies in order to reduce tax bills, particularly during inflationary periods. By contrast, in a Canadian tax case[8] LIFO was not acceptable for tax purposes. Thus, it is not allowed in several common law countries (including the United Kingdom). This has enabled the standard-setters to ban[9] LIFO without opposition from companies.

(b)   Goodwill. The United States standard-setters were able to require capitalization and amortization of goodwill in 1970.[10] In the United Kingdom, companies were fairly relaxed about such a proposal in the 1980s.[11] However, by 1990, there was fierce opposition, because goodwill was by then a major issue. By the end of 1995, there was still no revised United Kingdom exposure draft on this issue.

(c)   Deferred tax. There were British proposals[12] in 1975 to move to the then United States rules[13] involving full allocation of deferred tax. However, at the time the United Kingdom had a unique combination of high inflation, 100 per cent immediate tax depreciation for all plant and machinery, and an inventory appreciation relief which approximately allowed LIFO for tax purposes (without its being used for accounting purposes). This led to very large amounts of deferred tax and to overwhelming opposition to fully accounting for it.

Despite the unique events which caused such major international differences, the differences were very difficult to remove because of inertia, self-interest or national pride.

B. External influences

In many cases, a country's present accounting practices seem to be largely predictable from the influences of other countries in its history. For example:

(a)   The regulatory systems in Japan and the Republic of Korea for financial reporting by listed companies owe much to the influence of the United States after 1945;

(b)   All round the world, versions of British companies' legislation can be found in former colonies;

(c)   The distinguishing feature of French accounting regulation is the *plan comptable*. Belgium, Germany, Portugal and Spain, as well as a number of French-speaking African countries, have also adopted a *plan comptable*. A similar document - the chart of accounts - was used in the former Soviet Union and Central Europe; and a revised chart of accounts is still in use in the Commonwealth of Independent States.

In some cases, the accounting system which results may be inappropriate for a country's present needs, but as with differences stemming from unique events, those systems which result from external forces or from more subtle cultural influences may still be difficult to remove. Of course, some imported accounting systems may, nevertheless, be appropriate and be reinforced by other factors as explained immediately below.

C. Differing purposes

Perhaps the most fundamental of the causes of difference and therefore of the obstacles to harmonization is the existence of different purposes of financial reporting. A number of potentially competing purposes might exist, including the following:

(a) calculation of taxable income;

(b) control or encouragement of industry by the government;

(c) protection of creditors and the calculation of prudently distributable income;

(d) provision of information to management; and

(e) provision of information to outside shareholders in order to assist them with their financial decisions.

In all countries, the first of the above is an important use for accounting. Therefore, all governments will be interested in the accounting rules for at least this purpose. The key issue is whether there is a major competing purpose for accounting in a particular country. At this point, it is possible to divide much of the world into two groups of countries: those with substantial equity capital markets and those without. The latter countries have only one set of accounting rules, and these tend to be dominated by taxation rules and regulations. However, in other countries, there is a major competing purpose for financial reporting - that of serving capital markets. This leads to adjustments to the statutory accounts so that different information can be produced for the tax authorities and investors.

There is a substantial literature on the classification of countries by their systems of corporate financing.[14] The split into equity market and credit-based countries has been used in the study of economics, corporate governance and international accounting. As an example, one could look at the eight largest economies in Europe. These countries are partly chosen because of the availability of suitable statistics prepared on a comparable basis,[15] and because many other factors (such as political system and stage of economic development) can be held fairly constant. Some examples of the statistics are shown as tables 4.1 and 4.2, which reveal a remarkable scale of difference for these European Union member States. Although the cut-off may be difficult to determine, it is clear that the United Kingdom and the Netherlands have a greater reliance on equity and consequently less reliance on debt compared with Italy and Germany. Shareholdings can be examined in more detail[16] to show that Italian and German equity is dominated by "insiders" such as banks, governments or families, which have core holdings and seats on boards of directors and therefore little need for audited published financial reports. By contrast, there are large numbers of "outside" shareholders in the United Kingdom, including holdings by large institutions.

Use of similar statistics would show much of the world in the credit-based category (with Germany and Italy) but several countries in the equity market category (e.g. Australia, Canada, Singapore and the United States).

To conclude, equity market countries need financial reporting systems which serve millions of outside shareholders, who need different information from tax inspectors and governments, but cannot

Table 4.1. Domestic listed companies

Country	Per million of population (descending order)
United Kingdom	28.9
Netherlands	16.7
Belgium	16.3
Sweden	12.5
Spain	9.6
France	8.4
Germany	5.5
Italy	3.8

Sources: *World in Figures*, 1995, *The Economist*, London, 1994; *European Stock Exchange Statistics*, *Annual Report 1993*, *Federation of European Stock Exchanges*, Brussels, 1994.

Table 4.2. Market capitalization

Country	As a pecentage of GDP (descending order)
United Kingdom	137
Netherlands	61
Sweden	61
Belgium	38
France	37
Germany	26
Spain	24
Italy	14

Source: Centre for European Policy Studies, "Corporate Governance in Europe", June 1994.

be given all the internal information available to managers. Therefore, financial reporting using private sector accounting rules develops. Some typical features of the competing systems are suggested in table 4.3. These accounting differences seem to exist for a good reason, namely that they suit the economies they serve. This raises a major question about the feasibility of harmonization.

Table 4.3. Features of the two accounting models

Feature	Equity model	Credit/tax model
Tax influence (e.g. depreciation, asset valuation, bad debt provisions)	Many accounting rules separate from tax rules	Nearly all accounting rules and tax rules in conformity
Detailed accounting rules mostly by:	Bodies formally independent of government	Bodies formally controlled made by government
Accountancy profession	Relatively old and large	Relatively young and small
Status of consolidated financial statements	The only statement or the main statements	Regarded as supplementary or not available
Long-term contracts	Percentage of completion method	Completed contract method
Unsettled currency gains	Taken to income	Deferred
Legal reserves	Not found	Required
Profit and loss format	Expenses recorded by function (e.g. cost of sales)	Expenses recorded by nature (e.g. total wages)
Cash flow statements	Required	Not required, generally not found
Earnings per share disclosure	Required by listed companies	Not required, generally not found

D. Other factors

Many other factors have been suggested in the literature as causes of difference, and therefore obstacles to harmonization. These factors and the reasons for not including them above are as follows:

(a)   Language. It may be true that the use of certain languages is associated with certain features of accounting; for example, the *plan comptable* tends to be associated with French-speaking countries. However, this seems to be a result of auto-correlation, and is covered under "external influences" above. In another sense, language problems may slow down harmonization. For example, all of IASC's official output is in English only; however, this is probably not a major long-run problem.

(b)   Legal systems. For developed countries and for many others (e.g. South America and most of Africa), it is possible to split countries into codified legal systems and common law systems.[17] This is of great relevance to the regulatory system for accounting. However, there is a high degree of correlation between equity market countries and common law, and between creditor/tax countries and codified law.[18] On the whole, therefore, the same groupings would result. There are some exceptions - for example, the Netherlands has a codified legal system but an equity market history. However, its regulatory system and its accounting clearly fit the equity market model.[19] Therefore, it may not be useful to add legal systems to the causes of differences, although they may constitute an obstacle to change (see section IV).

(c) History/geography. These factors are too wide to be useful. The relevant features of history and geography are taken into account in other factors, such as accidents and external influence.

(d) Culture. Much interesting work has been done on the relationship between cultural variables and accounting differences.[20] It may be possible to use cultural differences to explain financing systems, legal systems, and so forth. However, it seems more useful for the purpose of this study to concentrate on the differences between the latter rather than the cultural variables behind them.

(e) Accountancy profession and education. International variations in the age, size and influence of the accountancy profession in different countries are very large. Undoubtedly, the legal system for setting accounting regulations has affected the development of the profession. Where rule-making remains in the hands of the government, the profession may remain small and underdeveloped. However, if the profession is small and underdeveloped, rule-making will certainly remain in governmental hands. The lack of a large educated profession may also slow down harmonization or any other progress in accounting.

E. Conclusions on country groups

It may be useful to propose four groups of countries with respect to probable reactions to international standards:

Group 1 - developed credit/tax countries. These would include Germany and Italy, as discussed earlier. One could also probably include Belgium, France, Greece, Portugal, Spain and Switzerland. These countries share codified legal systems and the importance of tax rules, and a comparatively small number of external auditors. The same could be said for Japan, whose apparently large equity markets are somewhat misleading because of the importance of cross-holdings. In nearly all ways, Japan fits into on the right-hand side of table 4.3.

Group 2 - former centrally planned economies. These include several in Eastern Europe (e.g. the Czech Republic, Poland and the Russian Federation). In Asia, one could possibly include Viet Nam and China, in the sense that their economies are being extensively liberalized. It seems likely that most of these countries will become similar to those in Group 1.

Group 3 - developed equity market countries. These countries include Australia, Canada, Ireland, the Netherlands, New Zealand, the United Kingdom and the United States. It may also be possible to include South Africa here. Nordic countries may also belong here, with Denmark the most easily included and Finland the least easily.

Group 4 - developing countries. Many countries in Africa, Asia and Latin America fit into this category. Frequently, the financial reporting system has been imported by a former colonial power, and it may not be entirely appropriate unless the related corporate financing system has also taken root. Nevertheless, in some countries strongly influenced by the Netherlands, the United Kingdom or the United States, the culture and economic facts may make Group 3 accounting appropriate. Of course, some of these countries (e.g. Singapore) are now "developed" in many ways, despite only a short period of independence.

III. SURVEYS OF COMPLIANCE

This section looks at past surveys of compliance with international accounting standards. It is important here to distinguish between *de jure* conformity (of the rules of a country with IASs) and *de facto* compliance (of the financial reporting of a particular company with IASs).

De jure conformity might refer to cases where (a) IASs and national rules are the same in all material respects; (b) IASs are less detailed than domestic rules or at least contain options that allow the domestic rules; or (c) IASs are more detailed than domestic rules and there are options in domestic rules that allow companies to follow IASs. Type (b) conformity is not very impressive and suggests that companies may be unaware of complying with IASs and that IASC had adjusted its standards to achieve this effect. This was the position for many English-speaking countries until 1995.

De facto compliance may be possible where (a) *de jure* conformity exists (e.g. in many English-speaking countries until 1995); (b) a country's rules are not very detailed (e.g. for group accounts in France or Switzerland); (c) there are no domestic rules (e.g. for group accounts in many developing countries); or (d) companies depart from domestic rules in order to comply with IASs (e.g. as seems to be likely for some group accounts of German listed companies from 1995).

It is obviously vital for the clarity of the discussion to distinguish between *de jure* conformity and *de facto* compliance, and preferably between the various types above.

IASC published its own survey[21] of *de jure* conformity with its standards in 1988. A revised version was completed in 1993, and therefore did not include the revised IAS 7 (cash flows) or the ten revised IASs which came into force in 1995. The two surveys had the following scopes:

Survey date	1988	1993
Countries covered	54	59
Number of IASs	29	29

A measure of the change in compliance over time can be gained from studying the aggregated scores for the 42 countries and the 23 IASs included in both surveys.[22] Table 4.4 shows the results of such calculations. The percentage figures for the rows were generally stable from 1988 to 1993 except that the "no requirement and non-conformity" row had noticeably decreased and the "national requirement developed separately but conforms" row had increased by about the same amount. If one looks at the rate of compliance using the first two rows, it can be said to have increased from 62 per cent to 70 per cent. This indicates an improvement in *de jure* conformity, and possibly in *de facto* compliance.

More precisely, in 1993 *de jure* conformity deliberately based on IASs was 24 per cent, but overall was 70 per cent. A further 16 per cent of country practices exhibited *de facto* compliance. If one assumed that *de jure* conformity was accompanied by *de facto* compliance (a heroic assumption), then *de facto* compliance was 86 per cent overall. However, there are several caveats to this, some already mentioned but included here for completeness:

(a)   The surveys were not up to date with IAS revisions of 1992 and onwards (or national revisions);

(b)   The scoring was done by member bodies, which might have given different interpretations to such words as "conforms in all material respects";

(c)   Some scores were missing from the data;

(d)   *De jure* conformity is not always accompanied by *de facto* compliance; and

(e)   *De jure* conformity or *de facto* compliance sometimes relates to the rules or practice of particular companies only (e.g. listed ones).

Table 4.4. Change in conformity with IASs, 1988-1993

Level of conformity	1988[22]		1993[23]	
IAS adopted as a national requirement or used as a basis for it[24]	211	(23%)	230	(24%)
National requirement developed separately and conforms in all material respects with IAS	363	(39%)	436	(46%)
No national requirement but national practice generally conforms with IAS	169	(18%)	147	(16%)
National requirement developed separately but does not conform with IAS	74	(8%)	75	(8%)
No national requirement and national practice does not generally conform with IAS	110	(12%)	53	(6%)
TOTAL	927	(100%)	941	(100%)

IV. THE UNCTAD SURVEY

An UNCTAD survey was carried out between May and August 1995 to update information on IASs. The responses to questions relating to conformity with international standards were compiled using 73 replies from 58 countries. Where there was more than one reply from a country (as for seven countries), a "main" respondent was selected (an official body in each case), with other replies used for confirmation and background.

In terms of coverage of the world, 48 of the 58 countries could easily be fitted into the four country groupings suggested at the end of section II (see table 4.5), although in the case of Group 4 this had been refined to refer particularly to developing countries strongly influenced by the United Kingdom, the United States or the Netherlands (i.e. Group 3). It should be noticed that the overwhelming majority of respondents from developing countries had this Group 3 background. This was unlikely to be due to language problems, as questionnaires were available in several languages (including Arabic, French and Spanish). It seemed more likely to be an illustration of the influences discussed in sections II and III, i.e. there were more accountants and there was more interest in financial reporting in Group 3 countries or those with Group 3 influence.

Many of the 10 countries in the residual Group 5 in table 4.5 could be classified in one of the four other groups, as suggested in section II. For example, China might fit into Group 2. However, the subsequent analysis will generally refer to the first four distinct groups, which cover 80 per cent of the countries responding.

Table 4.5. Groupings of respondents[25]

Group 1 (developed credit/tax)		Group 2 (former centrally planned economies)	
Belgium	Italy	Bulgaria	Lithuania
France	Japan	Czech Republic	Poland
Germany	Spain	Hungary	Romania
Greece	Switzerland	Latvia	Slovak Republic

Group 3 (developed equity markets) (a) (b)		Group 4 (countries with historical ties to the United Kingdom, the United States or the Netherlands)	
Australia	Denmark	Bangladesh	Nigeria
Canada	Finland	Botswana	Pakistan
Ireland	Sweden	Brazil	Papua New Guinea
Netherlands		Chile	Singapore
New Zealand		Cyprus	Solomon Islands
South Africa		India	Swaziland
United Kingdom		Indonesia	Thailand
United States		Jordan	United Republic of Tanzania
		Lesotho	Zambia
		Malawi	
		Malaysia	

Group 5 (residual)			
(a) Arabic	(b) South American	(c) Other	
Lebanon	Costa Rica	China	Democratic Republic of the
Morocco	Mexico	Republic of Korea	Congo
Sudan			Mali
			Turkey

A. *De jure* conformity with IASs

The survey asked a number of questions about whether a country's requirements conformed with IASs. As noted in section III, such *de jure* conformity could be divided into several types. For this section, the following distinctions between countries are useful:

Type A. National rules are generally as detailed as IASs and are based exactly or closely on them.

Type B. National rules are generally at least as detailed as IASs; and following the former generally leads to following the latter.

Type C. National rules are generally less detailed than IASs and leave scope for companies to follow the latter.

Type A conformity represents conscious efforts by the rule-makers. As noted earlier, Type B suggests "unintentional" *de facto* compliance by companies, although the rule-makers might have contributed by avoiding differences with IASs. If the national rules have non-IAS options in them, this might lead to some *de facto* non-compliance. In Type C countries, companies must consciously follow IASs for there to be *de facto* compliance.

For completeness, another type of country was added:

Type D. National rules do not comply with IASs in several important respects. Of course, companies in a Type D country can comply with IASs by producing supplementary financial statements.

The following are the predicted relationships between country groups and the types of IAS conformity discussed above:

Prediction (1) Developed credit/tax countries (Group 1) will tend towards Type D non-conformity with IASs because of a different philosophical basis for regulation and different purposes of financial reporting compared with IASC's. The same applies to former centrally planned countries (Group 2).

Prediction (2) Developed equity market countries (Group 3) and those influenced by them (Group 4) will tend to exhibit Types A to C conformity with IASs.

Prediction (3) In particular, Group 3a countries will tend to exhibit Type B "unintended" compliance because their rules are at least as detailed as, and often pre-date, IASC rules.

Prediction (4) By contrast, Group 4 countries will tend to exhibit Type A or C conformity because they find it efficient and politically acceptable to use IASs in place of former "colonial" rules.

Table 4.6 classifies countries[26] according to types of conformity on the basis of the answers to five of the questions in the questionnaire which concerned the detail of national rules and the degree to which national rules allowed IASs.

The findings show that all 45 countries[27] in Groups 1 to 4, except Switzerland, were classified in accordance with predictions into Type A, B, C or D. Switzerland was classified as a Type C country (rather than Type D) because its rules were sufficiently flexible to allow compliance with IASs, particularly for group financial statements. However, *de facto* compliance was restricted to a small group of companies. Concentration on group accounting only might allow some other Group 1 countries to be included as Type C (France, for example).

Turning to the more detailed findings, it may be seen that all Group 3a countries, except South Africa, were classified as Type B conformity. South Africa should perhaps have been classified as Group 4 (developing with United Kingdom/United States/Dutch influence), which would have removed this slight anomaly. Furthermore, all 21 Group 4 countries were classified as Types A or C.

In summary, the findings show that if a country could be clearly classified into one of Groups 1 to 4 in table 4.5, then a confident prediction could be made about its degree of *de jure* conformity with IASs. The caveats to the extension of this are that this sample of countries might not have been representative of the whole world. For example, it has already been mentioned that there were very few French-speaking developing countries among the respondents. However, even this allowed a prediction: that they were not Type A or B countries, which was why they did not feel inclined to reply to a questionnaire related to IASC.

Incidentally, the questionnaire responses (leading to allocation to types) from those countries that were difficult to classify (i.e. shown as Group 5) in table 4.5 could be rationalized in several cases:

(a) China as Type D because it is generally centrally planned;
(b) Mali as Type D because of French colonial influence; and
(c) Thailand as Type C because of the influence of the United Kingdom and the United States.

Table 4.6. *De jure* conformity

Type A: **National rules comply or mostly comply** (total = 17)
Botswana, Brazil, Chile, Cyprus, Indonesia, Jordan, Lesotho, Malawi, Nigeria, Pakistan, Singapore, Zambia, Zimbabwe (Group 4);
Costa Rica, Mexico (Group 5b)
Republic of Korea, Turkey (Group 5c)

Type B: **Detailed national rules** (total = 8)
Australia, Canada, Ireland, Netherlands, New Zealand, United Kingdom, United States (Group 3a);
Sweden (Group 3b)

Type C: **Less detailed national rules** (total = 14)
Switzerland (Group 1;)
Lithuania (Group 2);
South Africa (Group 3a);
Denmark, Finland (Group 3b);
Bangladesh, India, Malaysia, Papua New Guinea, Solomon Islands, Swaziland, United Republic of Tanzania (Group 4);
Lebanon (Group 5a);
Thailand (Group 5c)

Type D: **National rules do not comply or partially comply** (total = 15)
Belgium, France, Germany, Greece, Italy, Japan, Spain (Group 1);
Czech Republic, Hungary, Poland, Romania (Group 2);
Sudan (Group 5a)
China, Democratic Republic of the Congo, Mali, (Group 5c)

B. *De facto* compliance with IASs

Compliance with IASs in practice for financial reporting by companies can occur in a country if one of the following applies (using the country types from above). There can be compliance in:

(a)   Type A countries, to the extent that companies in practice follow national rules. One could expect that at least listed companies and those with international connections do this;

(b)   Type B countries in general (with the caveat that certain national options might be inconsistent with IASs, particularly those from 1995 onwards);

(c)   Type C countries, in those cases (which may be unusual) where companies choose to comply with IASs; and

(d)   Type D countries, where certain companies (generally the group accounts of a few listed companies) choose to comply with IASs in their statutory financial statements (where this would be legal) or in supplementary statements.

The questionnaire asked for information on *de facto* use of IASs, and table 4.7 shows the results for the relevant groups of countries, excluding Type A (which used IASs anyway) and Type B (where companies unconsciously complied). As may be seen, there was some use of IASs in nearly all Type C countries and in most Type D countries. Such use was generally confined to listed companies (or companies with publicly traded securities) in many such countries. On the whole, use of IASs was a minority practice even for consolidated accounting by listed companies.

Type B countries (mostly corresponding to developed equity market countries) reported some deliberate compliance by companies in addition to "unintended" compliance. For example, several Canadian companies quoted on the Toronto Stock Exchange stated that they complied with IASs.

Table 4.7.   Use of IASs by companies (no. of countries)

	Type C countries	Type D countries
General use of IASs* where national rules are silent or flexible	6	1
Use of IASs* by a few companies with international interests**	4	5
Use of IASs* for supplementary reports by a few companies**	4	7
No direct use of IASs	1	6
Total countries	14	18

*   In each case, group accounting was specified.
**   One Type C country and one Type D country reported both of these, hence the totals did not appear to add up correctly.

C. Conformity related to equity markets

The questionnaire asked for data relating to the perceived purpose of annual financial statements. Since this was the most subjective area of the questionnaire, the results must be treated with caution. However, the data can be used to check the link between strong equity markets and a certain type of accounting.   Expressed in terms of this section's terminology, investment decisions by shareholders would be expected to be the major use of financial statements in Group 3 countries (but not in Group 1 or Group 2 countries) and this would be associated with requirements for an IASC style of reporting (i.e. Type A or B conformity).

Respondents were asked to rank nine potential objectives of the annual reports of quoted companies.   One of the objectives related to use by shareholders for investment decisions (others concerned dividends, tax, management, etc.). The relationship to country groupings could be expressed as follows:

Prediction (5)   Shareholder investment decisions are seen as a more important use in equity market countries (Group 3) than in creditor/tax countries (Group 1) or former centrally planned economies (Group 2).

Prediction (6)   Shareholder investment decisions are seen as a more important use in IAS - conforming countries (Types A to C) than in non-conforming countries (Type D).

The average rank for shareholder decisions (out of a potential score of 9, 1 was the highest rank and 9 the lowest) is shown in table 4.8, by groups of countries (as in table 4.5) and by types of compliance (as in table 4.6). It can be seen that the Group 3 average rank was above the Groups 1 and 2 average ranks, while the average rank for Type D was the lowest for any type. To provide greater detail, Group 5(b) (South America) is also included in Table 4.8. The rank shown for South America, remarkably higher than for creditor/tax countries (Group 1), suggests that these two groups are now noticeably different, even though strongly linked by history.

Table 4.8. User rank for investment decisions by shareholders

Country groupings	Average rank
1 - Developed creditor/tax	4.67
2 - Former centrally planned	2.00
3a- Equity market	1.13
3b- Equity market	1.00
4 - Developing countries	2.18
5b- South America	1.5

Compliance types	
A - IASs	2.17
B - Detailed rules	1.00
C - Less detailed rules	1.50
D - Non-compliance	2.94

V. CONCLUSIONS, PROSPECTS AND PROPOSALS

A. Conclusions on conformity

Deliberate *de jure* conformity with IASs was exhibited by about a quarter of the countries for which survey data allowed clear classification. These countries (called Type A in section IV) are mostly former British colonies. It is known[28] that Hong Kong, for which there was no survey data, also fits into this category. In the countries in this group, the local accountancy bodies are members of IASC, and it is, therefore, politically acceptable as well as efficient to adopt or adapt IASs as national practice. This helps to avoid the creation of unintended differences.

Several Arab countries with strong ties to the United States or the United Kingdom also base their accounting standards closely on those of IASC. These countries include Jordan, Saudi Arabia and the United Arab Emirates.

Some other countries (Type B) exhibited *de jure* conformity in the sense that although their accounting rules are in many cases more detailed than IASs and might have pre-dated them, they are consistent with IASs or allow IASs to be followed. These countries are generally developed capital-market countries. The main rule-makers here are typically private sector standard-setters who feel uncomfortable when their rules depart from those of IASC, even if the standard-setters are not professional accountancy bodies and therefore not members of IASC or its Board. For example, the United States Financial Accounting Standards Board's mission statement includes the aim to "promote the international comparability of accounting standards". The United Kingdom's Accounting Standards Board also takes account of international developments and supports the IASC,[29] preferring to avoid differences from IASs. For example, in 1995 two major areas of United Kingdom difference from IASC proposals (goodwill and deferred tax) were under review, and international comparisons are always examined in the discussion documents and so forth. In Australia, the standard-setters announced in September 1995 that their standards would be modified to ensure that compliance with them would ensure compliance with IASs.

A third group of countries (Type C) has less detailed rules than IASs, and the rules generally allow IASs to be followed. There is a greater chance here for the rules not to be followed *de facto*. In terms of the survey these countries include many former British colonies, but also Denmark, Finland and Switzerland.

The fourth group of countries (Type D) have rules noticeably different from IASs, which makes *de facto* compliance unlikely or impossible without a separate set of IAS financial statements. The creditor/tax countries included here are perhaps reluctant to fully endorse and/or comply with IASs because of a perceived bias toward Anglo-Saxon accounting.[30] However, IASs have been important for various purposes, for example:

(a)   Italy has used IASs for consolidated accounting for listed companies since the late 1970s. CONSOB[31] requires special reporting and auditing for these companies;

(b)   Several French companies have used IASs for group accounting, for which French law specifically allows various departures from normal French rules;

(c)   A surprising development in Germany in 1995 saw Bayer and Schering preparing group accounts in conformity with IASs as well as German rules. This was followed by an announcement from the Ministry of Justice that they would allow the use by listed companies of IASs for group accounts even if this led to departure from German rules;

(d)   The Japanese Ministry of Finance (which controls the group accounts of publicly traded companies) has made some encouraging remarks about IASs and has agreed to examine whether existing Japanese differences need to be maintained.

Type D also includes former and current centrally planned economies. In most of Eastern Europe, the influence of EC Directives was more noticeable than that of IASs because of technical cooperation activities and growing trade and investment. However, there was a chance that some of the Asian countries would become equity market countries with financial reporting based more generally on IASs. It should be noted that the Hong Kong Society of Accountants announced in 1993 that it would base its standards in future on IASs, not on the standards of the United Kingdom.

The attitude of rule-makers in these countries to IASs was also of interest. A further source of data on this subject was responses to the survey question which asked about the account taken of IASs by the country's main regulators. Table 4.9 shows the position for 41 of the countries. Across the groups, there was a remarkable increase in the importance of IASs to the main rule-makers. Nevertheless, it is interesting that the majority of creditor/tax and former centrally planned countries reported a desire to avoid differences from the IASC.

De facto compliance with IASs was substantial for the types of enterprises that followed national rules in Type A countries and (unintentionally) for most companies in Type B countries, at least until 1995 when ten revised IASs came into force. In many Type C countries, IASs were followed by rule-

Table 4.9.   Attitude of main rule-makers to IASs (using groups* from table 4.5)

Economies	No account of IASs	IAS is background but not closely followed	Effort is made to avoid differences	Rules based on IASs
Developed creditor/tax	0	3	5	0
Former centrally planned **	0	1	5	1
Developed equity market	0	0	8	0
Developing countries ***	0	0	1	17
Totals	0	4	19	18

*   The Nordic countries (Group 3b) were omitted because there is mixed regulation. Group 5 was also omitted because it is a residual.
**   One further country had an unclear score.
***   United Kingdom/United States and Netherlands influence

makers or by certain companies. In Type D countries, compliance was confined to the consolidated accounts of most or a few listed companies.

B. Conclusions on obstacles to international accounting standards

The obstacles to the adoption of international standards are related to the causes of differences and to the types of country, as examined in sections I to III. In summary:

In developing countries with a background of Netherlands/United Kingdom/United States involvement, there are few obstacles to *de jure* conformity. The legal system generally delegates standard-setting to the private sector, and accounting philosophy is already similar to that of IASC. Existing rules are not so well developed as to stand in the way of adopting IASs. Perhaps the main problem here is educational. There might be insufficient training of accountants or auditors to enable universal use of IASs.

In developed equity market countries, the main obstacle to the adoption of IASs is that national rules were older, more detailed and entrenched. In contrast, IASs were seen as too broad and containing too many alternatives. The rule-makers in these countries have thought that the superiority of national rules justifies accounting differences. Also, the rule-makers are subject to competing interests. Many entrenched differences seem to result from unique events in the past.

In developed creditor/tax countries, the obstacle is that the main purpose of accounting is not that assumed by IASC, so that IASs might be thought inappropriate for most domestic purposes. Governments are the main rule-makers and they are greatly interested neither in international comparisons nor in IASC. As in other developed countries, national practices are entrenched. In this case, there is the added problem that governments change rules slowly and infrequently.

In former centrally planned economies, some of the same features can be found as in creditor/tax countries. However, these countries are involved in radical change, and so they are more likely to be open to the use of international standards.

Most other countries could be approximately fitted into one of the above four groups, although South American countries seem to show similarities with both equity market and creditor/tax countries.

A further potential obstacle to the use of international standards is that accounting rules in some countries might be constrained by external forces. For example, the company law directives of the European Council are now legally binding on governments in the 15 countries of the European Union and a few others.[32] There are probably few, if any, difficulties[33] at present resulting for IAS compliance, although this was not the case for some national laws based on the directives. However, as IASs change in the light of new circumstances or new thinking, they may become inconsistent with directives. An example of potential difficulty is "marking to market" for certain investments.[34]

C. Prospects

The prospects for international standards also seem to vary with the type of country.

For Type A countries (national rules conform or almost conform), IASs are in many cases already established. It seems likely that more of them will follow this trend, especially as the countries develop and as globalization of markets proceeds. A proposal for improvement is to ensure that such countries feel involved in IASC. This is already happening, with Malaysia, Sri Lanka and Zimbabwe joining the

Board in 1995 and with a project on agriculture having been added to IASC's work programme. Assistance with education in these countries would further the use of IASs.

For Type B countries (detailed national rules), *de jure* conformity actually decreased in 1995 as revised IASs came into force. However, most such countries are closely involved in the work of IASC and are likely to try to remove national differences as regards IASs in due course. As IASs move towards becoming a world standard, large companies might begin to lobby against differences from IASs rather than for special national practices. This will become even more likely if the IOSCO/IASC plans succeed in making IASs acceptable for cross-border listings, particularly for the purposes of the New York Stock Exchange.

For Type C countries (less detailed national rules), the prospects for use of IASs are good in that national rules may remain less detailed than IASs or may be based on the latter. In some cases, IASs may be required or chosen for specific purposes only, such as the consolidated reports of listed companies.

For Type D countries (national rules do not comply), the prospects for generalized use of IASs in the short or medium term do not appear to be good. The speed at which the formerly centrally planned economies adopt international standards depends on their economic conditions, the amount of technical assistance and the level of accounting education and retraining. Nevertheless, there are already some uses of IASs, particularly for raising international capital.

The key factor regarding these uses is that they concern the group accounts of listed companies. Of course, it is the listed companies in these countries which best fit the equity market model, and it is their group accounts which are of interest to the market. Since the group accounts are not relevant for tax or dividend distribution, published consolidated financial reporting of listed companies could use international standards. This would leave the accounts of non-listed companies unaffected, thus concentrating the costs and benefits of harmonization in the relevant area.

Momentum is building to use international accounting standards. There is a mood for change in the EU to back IASC, particularly for this purpose. In early 1996, EU governmental representatives under the leadership of EC officials investigated the incompatibilities between EC Directives and IASs. The objective was to remove any such problems by changing either the directives or the IASs, so that the EU could then wholeheartedly support IASC. One of the motivations was the belief that otherwise, United States rules may become the world standard, thereby reducing European influence. It was found that there were no major conflicts between EC Directives and IASs. Members of the EU which are credit/tax countries, such as France and Germany, are allowing use of IASs for the consolidated accounts of listed companies. This shows that a consensus is building. Thus, countries which are apparently different are adopting similar solutions. Of course, the success of the IOSCO/IASC project would enhance the prospect of world standards led by IASC. In addition, the WTO's Working Party on Professional Services is cooperating with and encouraging the efforts of IASC and IOSCO to formulate international accounting standards aimed at achieving greater comparability in financial statements and facilitating the effective liberalization of accountancy services.

Notes

1   This chapter was prepared with the assistance of Professor C.W. Nobes, University of Reading, United Kingdom.

2   See *International Accounting and Reporting Issues: 1990 Review* (New York and Geneva: United Nations, Sales No.E.91.II.A.3), chap.3.

3   *Conclusions on Accounting and Reporting by Transnational Corporations* (New York and Geneva: United Nations, 1994, Sales No. E.94.II.A.9).

4   The country members are accountancy bodies appointed by IFAC. Some of the "countries" are in fact groups (e.g. the Nordic Federation of Public Accountants).

5   Other jurisdictions (e.g. Singapore) had already done this.

6   For consolidated financial statements.

7   IASs 3 and 6, and IAS 15, respectively. IAS 15 does not have to be followed for compliance with international standards to be claimed.

8   Minister of National Revenue v. Anaconda American Brass Ltd. (1956), AC 85.

9   Statement of Standard Accounting Practice (SSAP) 9 suggests that LIFO will not enable a true and fair view to be given, and would thus be illegal in the United Kingdom.

10   Accounting Principles Board (APB) Opinion 17.

11   See C.W. Nobes, "A political history of goodwill in Britain: An illustration of cyclical standard setting", *Abacus*, September 1992.

12   Statement of Standard Accounting Practice (SSAP) 11, which was withdrawn before it became operative.

13   Accounting Principles Board (APB) Opinion 11.

14   E.g. J. Zysman, *Governments, Markets and Growth: Financial Systems and the Politics of Industrial Change* (New York: Cornell University Press, 1983); J. Franks and C. Mayer, "Corporate Control: A Synthesis of the International Evidence", working paper of the London Business School, 1992; C. W. Nobes and R. H. Parker, *Issues in Multinational Accounting* (Oxford: Philip Allan, 1988), p. 31.

15   More statistics are used by C.W. Nobes in "Corporate Financing and Its Effects on European Accounting Differences", Reading University Discussion Papers, 1995.

16   Federation of European Stock Exchanges, *Share Ownership Structure in Europe*, Brussels, 1993.

17   R. David and J. E. C. Brierley, *Major Legal Systems in the World Today*,(London: Stephens, 1985).

18   C. W. Nobes and R. H. Parker, *Comparative International Accounting*, (Hemel Hempstead: Prentice Hall, 1995), chap. 1.

19   S. A. Zeff, F. van der Wel and K. Camfferman, *Company Financial Reporting: A Historical and Comparative Study of the Dutch Regulatory Process*, (Amsterdam, North-Holland, 1992).

20   E.g. S. J. Gray, "Towards a theory of cultural influence on the development of accounting systems internationally", *Abacus*, March 1988.

21   IASC, *Survey of Use and Application of International Accounting Standards*, 1988.

22   This excludes IASs 3 and 6, which were withdrawn by 1993, and IAS 15, which was non-mandatory.

23   The totals do not agree with the number of countries (42) multiplied by the number of standards included (23), because several scores were missing.

24   This is a conflation of two headings in the survey.

25   These groupings have been made solely for the purposes of this report.

26   There are 54 countries shown in table 4.6. This excludes Bulgaria, Latvia, Morocco and the Slovak Republic, which were difficult to classify according to types of conformity from the data in the questionnaires.

27   There are 48 countries in Groups 1 to 4, but Bulgaria, Latvia and the Slovak Republic were difficult to classify, as explained in footnote 24.

28   T. E. Cooke and R. H. Parker, *Financial Reporting in the West Pacific Rim* (London: Routledge, 1994).

29   Accounting Standard Board, "Foreword to Accounting Standards" (London, 1993), para. 36.

30   H. Kleekämper, "IASC: Das trojanische Pferd der SEC", in W. Ballwieser, *US-amerikanische Rechnungslegung* (Stuttgart, Schäffer-Poeschel Verlag, 1995).

31   Commissione Nazionale per le Società e la Borsa. IASs have been used to fill in gaps where there are no Italian rules. However, a revised civil code came into force for 1994, and reduced the scope for use of IASs.

32   E.g. Norway, as a member of the European Economic Area.

33   FEE, *Seventh Directive Options and Their Implementation* (London: Routledge, 1993), chap. 4.

34   This is a potential IAS development, and creates legal problems under the Fourth Directive.

CHAPTER V

REDUCING BARRIERS TO TRADE IN ACCOUNTING SERVICES AND THE DEVELOPMENT OF A BENCHMARK FOR PROFESSIONAL QUALIFICATIONS

SUMMARY AND CONCLUSIONS

The World Trade Organization and its Working Party on Professional Services have taken up the question of reducing barriers to trade in accountancy services. UNCTAD, for its part, is developing a benchmark for evaluating professional qualifications. This work now has a double significance, since the development of a benchmark for professional qualifications would both strengthen the profession in developing countries and allow those countries to take advantage of any reductions in the barriers to trade in accountancy services. This is in line with the outcome of UNCTAD IX, where UNCTAD was urged to extend appropriate technical assistance to developing countries to strengthen their service sectors and help them reap the maximum possible benefits from liberalization of trade in services.

The representative of the **United Kingdom** suggested that initiatives relating to international education should have full regard to the work of the International Federation of Accountants (IFAC) in this area. The representative of the **World Trade Organization** confirmed that there was no duplication in the work of its Working Party and UNCTAD.

ISAR noted that it was now clear that there would be no duplication between UNCTAD and WTO and that work would proceed on the development of a benchmark for professional qualifications, as requested by ISAR at its eleventh session and subsequently approved by its parent bodies.

I. THE MANDATE OF THE WORKING PARTY ON PROFESSIONAL SERVICES

The World Trade Organization (formerly the General Agreement on Trade and Tariffs -GATT) established the Working Party on Professional Services (the Working Party or WPPS). The Decision on Professional Services required the Working Party to make recommendations on the disciplines needed to ensure that measures relating to qualification requirements and procedures, technical standards and licensing requirements in the field of professional services did not constitute unnecessary barriers to trade. The Decision then singled out work in the accountancy sector as a matter of priority. Paragraph 2 of the Decision identified the following broad areas where the Working Party was to concentrate its efforts and to make recommendations to the Council on Trade in Services:

- development of multilateral disciplines to ensure that regulatory requirements are (a) objective and transparent criteria, such as competence and the ability to supply the service; and (b) not more burdensome than necessary to ensure quality, and not a restriction on supply;
- using international standards and, in doing so, encouraging the cooperation with the relevant international organizations as defined under General Agreement on Trade in Services (GATS) Article VI, paragraph 5(b), so as to give full effect to Article VII, paragraph 5;
- facilitating the effective application of Article VI, paragraph 6, by establishing guidelines for the recognition of qualifications.

In elaborating these disciplines, the Working Party was to take account of the importance of the governmental and non-governmental bodies regulating professional services. One of the reasons why the accounting profession was chosen by the Working Party to start its work was that it is large, relatively mobile, and highly regulated to protect the public by ensuring the quality of the service. The specific regulatory requirements will continue to be set by governments and reasonable local requirements will not be overridden by the WTO process. However, that WTO process would indirectly promote the harmonization or convergence of regulatory regimes.

II. THE WORKING PARTY'S ACTIVITIES

A. Past meetings

The Working Party has met six times: in July and October 1995, and January, March, July and October 1996. The first meeting (July) developed an understanding of the workload and priorities. At the second meeting (October) the members familiarized themselves with the organization and regulation of the accountancy profession. Material was presented from various organizations. The representative of the Organisation for Economic Co-operation and Development (OECD) made a presentation of its inventory of measures affecting the trade in professional services. The inventory1 was comprehensive and covers (i) the conditions of access to a profession/professional title in each OECD country; (ii) the scope of activities exercised by each profession; and (iii) measures relevant to foreign firms and natural persons.

A representative of the International Federation of Accountants (IFAC) made a presentation during a seminar organized outside the session on the status of the accounting profession as reported by 49 of its member bodies. The report[2] covered a variety of IFAC members, including the following developing countries and countries in transition: Brazil, Dominican Republic, Egypt, Hungary, Kenya, Malaysia, Mexico, Nigeria, Philippines, Poland, South Africa, Swaziland, Taiwan Province of China, Thailand, Uruguay and Zimbabwe. However, this report, although quite representative from a geographical viewpoint, was not sufficiently representative. In particular, Arab countries, China, French-speaking Africa and the Indian subcontinent were absent from the survey.

Lastly, UNCTAD made a presentation on ISAR, a summary of its activities and its interest in developing a benchmark for professional qualifications and a system for accreditation.

At the third meeting (January) of the Working Party a list of issues was produced for future consideration. The delegations noted that further analytical information was needed on the regulatory regimes of developing countries. It was decided that a focused questionnaire on specific aspects of domestic regulations which affect the accountancy sector should be formulated and circulated. At the same time, substantive work by the WPPS should begin on the elaboration of multilateral disciplines to ensure that the regulatory regimes do not act as barriers to trade.

The Chairperson of the Working Party requested the WTO secretariat to provide information on the relevance of certain existing GATT instruments to the Working Party's mandate, namely the Agreement on Technical Barriers to Trade and the Agreement on Import Licensing Procedures. The first agreement ensures that technical regulations and standards, as well as certification procedures, do not create unnecessary obstacles to the trade in goods, and considers what constitutes "unnecessary obstacles" to trade and hence would be relevant to the discussion of technical and conceptual issues with respect to accountancy. The second agreement requires that national licensing procedures are not more burdensome than necessary for administering a licensing system, and that they are transparent and predictable and protect foreign suppliers from unnecessary delays and arbitrary actions.

At the fourth meeting (18 March 1996) the questionnaire was approved to collect additional information. It contains nearly 40 questions and is broken down into the following issues:

1. general questions on matters such as professional titles, scope of service and professional bodies;
2. qualification requirements;
3. technical standards and ethics;
4. licensing requirements and procedures;
5. recognition of qualifications;
6. regulations governing the establishment of a commercial presence;
7. regulations governing the entry and temporary stay of natural persons for the purpose of supplying accountancy services; and
8. nationality and residence requirements.

As previously mentioned, the Working Party initially received little information on many of the developing countries and countries in transition. At its request, UNCTAD provided the report in chapter VI. It presents information on qualification and licensing requirements which has been collected over the years through ISAR questionnaires. This information was updated where possible. UNCTAD appreciates the assistance of respondents in updating this information. Eventually, WTO received 11 responses to its questionnaire from developing countries, out of a total of 23 replies.

B. Priorities of the Working Party

During the third and fourth meetings a number of issues were proposed for consideration by the Working Party at its fifth meeting to be held in July 1996:

1. qualification requirements and procedures;
2. licensing requirements (other than qualification requirements) and procedures;
3. regulations governing the establishment of a commercial presence;
4. nationality/citizenship/residence requirements;
5. professional liability/ethics;
6. regulations governing entry and temporary stay of natural persons for the purpose of supplying accountancy services;
7. establishing guidelines for the recognition of qualifications; and
8. use of international accounting standards.

As yet, the Working Party has not set priorities for the order in which the issues identified above will be addressed. Initial topics may include the differences and similarities of individuals and firms in public practice and existing multilateral guidelines. In this regard it was decided to invite the International Accounting Standards Committee to make a presentation on its activities. ISAR's paper on "Compliance with International Accounting Standards" was made available to the Working Party.

III. THE RELATIONSHIP BETWEEN THE WORK OF ISAR AND THAT OF WPPS

A. General remarks

The UNCTAD secretariat has responded to the above-mentioned request for information by the Working Party and will continue to attend meetings in the capacity of observer, which essentially places ISAR in a consultative position. However, ISAR could have more of an impact on the deliberations and recommendations of the Working Party if its members actively participate in the Working Party as part of their country delegations. At least two ISAR members have attended meetings of the Working Party as part of their country delegations.

Also, it is proposed that UNCTAD hold informal briefing sessions for developing countries on issues under consideration by WTO. Two such sessions - on the composition, work and regulation of the profession - have been held.

ISAR has proposed developing an international benchmark for professional qualifications and a system of accreditation. Given the emergence of the Working Party and the impending freer international market for accountancy services, the need to be able to assess the skills of potential service providers by means of some established benchmark is now apparent. The development of a benchmark and an accreditation system by UNCTAD would not duplicate the work of WTO since it is not the task of the Working Party to develop standards; but WTO could encourage their use once developed. The Working Party's mandate refers to international standards which cover three categories: auditing standards, accounting standards and education and ethical standards.

According to Article VII (1) and (5) of the General Agreement on Trade in Services:

"A member may recognize the education or experience obtained, requirements met or licences or certifications granted in a particular country...Wherever appropriate, recognition should be based on multilaterally agreed criteria. In appropriate cases, Members shall work in cooperation with relevant intergovernmental and non-governmental organizations towards the establishment and adoption of common international standards and criteria for recognition and common international standards for the practice of relevant services, trades and professions."

This language would give ample justification for UNCTAD to finally take up ISAR's request regarding the development of a benchmark for professional qualifications and certification system. However, ISAR members must also work to ensure that the benchmark and certification system gains acceptance by the government and the profession if WPPS is to take note of this development.

B. The proposed project for development of a benchmark for a professional qualification and a certification system

1. Background

The origin of this proposal was the 1991 Dakar Conference on Accountancy Development in Africa. The Conference proposed that to impart more value to African diplomas the Education Committee of IFAC could review the curricula of selected African universities and institutes to see whether they met its international educational guidelines. If they did, the committee could "attest" that the programme complied with its guidelines. Some institutes could be certified right away; to promote certification, the Education Committee could put together teams of experts who would train trainers in curriculum development and materials development.

At its eleventh session (1993) ISAR considered the state of accounting education worldwide. It found that while accounting education was not coping fully with the constantly changing environment, it was falling further behind in developing countries. It decided that the profession needed to work towards reducing the education gap between the developed and the developing world. The Chairman of the eleventh session, Mr. Talal Abu-Ghazaleh (Jordan), proposed a master plan for accounting education and certification. The objective would be to progressively narrow the standards gap between developed and developing nations to an acceptable size. There was a need to develop a benchmark which could be used by developing countries to assess their national qualifications. This would close the gap and make the accounting profession more equal around the world.

While in many countries a high level of accountancy has been achieved, there is no globally accepted level. This poses problems for developing countries and countries in transition in which accountants are not accepted equally. One expert from an EU country suggested that a new designation should be established, that of United Nations registered accountant. Recognizing that the education gap was far more serious worldwide than had hitherto been recognized by the profession, and also recognizing the need to develop a benchmark, ISAR concluded its discussion by calling upon the International Federation of Accountants to take up this task. Specifically, it asked the Federation to develop qualification standards for accountants and auditors which could be endorsed by the United Nations. At the twelfth session, IFAC replied that such a task was beyond its resources and mandate. However, it did subsequently issue a policy statement on the "Recognition of Professional Accountancy Qualifications".

To move the exercise forward, ISAR asked that the feasibility of an accreditation system be investigated by the secretariat. However, initiatives in this respect were postponed by the Commission on International Investment and Transnational Corporations. The Commission felt that given the emergence of the WTO, and in particular the attention which would be given to trade in services, any activities by ISAR in this respect would be premature and could lead to a duplication of efforts.

However, in anticipation that ISAR would continue with the project, an ad hoc meeting of select members of the Group was held in November 1994 to consider, amongst other issues, how such a project might be undertaken. The primary question which this meeting debated was the level within the accountancy profession (accounting technicians, management accountants, accountants or auditors in professional public practice) to which the project would be directed. The consensus was that the feasibility study for developing a benchmark and an accreditation system should be assessed more comprehensively. It should consider the possibility of implementing a programme at the highest professional level - that of public accountancy. However, at the thirteenth session of ISAR, it was decided that the benchmark/certification system should also be developed for management and financial accountants.

A distinction should be made between management and financial accountants on the one hand and accountants in public practice on the other. In certain Western European countries, Germany for instance, the only accountants recognized as such are those in public practice. Management and financial functions are not provided by professionals called accountants, but rather by those with commercial degrees and relevant experience. In other West European countries, including the United Kingdom, accountants fulfil both functions but require a special licence to undertake public practice. In countries such as Germany, those who leave public practice are also deemed to have left the profession. In other countries, such as the United Kingdom, those not in public practice are still deemed to be part of the profession so long as they are members of one of the professional accountancy bodies. Such members will have gained the same qualification as members in public practice but will not hold a licence to practise. Licensing requirements are additional and may involve an extra level of testing.

In order to facilitate the transfer of professionals between countries, the chief need is to achieve mutual recognition of those in public practice. Those not in public practice require no special recognition and indeed only have to find a job in order to work anywhere in the world; but some form of accreditation would strengthen the credibility of the accountancy qualifications of non-practising accountants. It would facilitate the mutual recognition of qualifications if there was some benchmark against which all professional qualifications could be compared. This benchmark qualification should cover public practice. If it also covered management and finance, this would be an additional benefit. In addition to a benchmark standard, there would have to be an accreditation system for certifying whether qualifications met the benchmark. Lastly, there would need to be local tests in tax and law.

Ongoing discussions between UNCTAD and WTO staff members on the development of a benchmark/certification system have established that the WTO does not consider the activity to be within its mandate. The Working Party should have a keen interest in the project in view of its relevance to the activities of the WTO. To decrease trade barriers in accounting services, it could recommend the use of international standards for accounting, auditing and education. In conformity with the nature of multilateral instruments, the Working Party could not require the use of international standards. However, it is obvious that if countries used international standards in recognizing qualifications, the costs of the process of granting recognition would be considerably reduced. This is particularly important for developing countries which might not have mature professional associations that could assist their governments in this process.

2. Justification for the project

For a number of years ISAR has been concerned with the level of development of accountancy and accountancy education and training throughout the world and has researched the subject thoroughly.[3] Developing countries have a great shortage of qualified accountants, which has a considerable impact upon accountability within these countries. Furthermore, it is a mandate of the Division on Investment, Technology and Enterprise Development to promote foreign direct investment as a mechanism for development. All too often, because of the lack of adequate financial information, potential investors are understandably reluctant to invest. Almost every study of the quality of accounting and management information systems in developing countries has confirmed the correlation between the level of economic development and accounting development. If the financial management system is primitive, there can be no effective resource allocation or project management.

Poor accounting, budgeting and auditing erode the performance of development programmes. Failure and inability to account effectively for limited resources in Africa, for instance, have contributed greatly to the current problems of the continent. Such failure or inability has been attributed, in part, to the lack of competent accounting personnel.

The need for effective and efficient accounting systems and practices is also generated by the increase in the volume of financial transactions arising from new economic cooperation among developing and transitional countries, and by the proliferation of business enterprises, joint ventures, and bilateral and multilateral trade pacts.

A sustainable answer to the problem would involve tackling it from both the demand and the supply side. Too often, the demand for qualified accountants in developing and transitional countries is met by foreign accountants through the networks of the major international accountancy firms or to a lesser extent by nationals with foreign accountancy qualifications. Some professionals, particularly from East Africa and Eastern Europe, have developed sound accountancy skills and have created admirable professional accountancy organizations. Yet transnational corporations often overlook the local skills in favour of those imported through international accountancy firms. This effectively "downgrades" the local profession. Talented and ambitious locals are forced to seek Western accountancy qualifications which, owing to economic constraints, are often unattainable. The profession in many developing and transitional countries is effectively segregated into a two-tier structure, with all the lucrative and prestigious engagements undertaken by Western experts. This project could indirectly remedy this inequity by allowing the qualifications of national professionals to be assessed. In the short run, this would tackle the "perception" problem and increase the value of qualified indigenous accountants. However, it must be kept in mind that this solution has a long-term perspective and is still dependent on an increase in the overall supply of qualified accountants, who would in turn benefit from greater recognition of their qualifications.

3. *Feasibility of a benchmark and certification system*

The feasibility of a benchmark and certification system has been analysed by the UNCTAD secretariat and the following factors should now be discussed:

(a)   There would be great difficulty in setting the appropriate level for the qualification: too high a level would lead to the exclusion of many developing countries because they do not have the facilities locally to train accountants to a high standard, and too low a level would cause the qualification to lack credibility. However, IFAC has developed the necessary elements for a qualification in its policy statement and these should be assessed in terms of whether they form an appropriate level for an international benchmark. The Association of Chartered Certified Accountants (ACCA) is considering converting its UK-based qualification to an internationally based one. It is important to note that large numbers of accountants from developing countries have already earned the ACCA qualification and it appears to be set at a realistic level. Even if the level of the qualification poses no problems, it would be necessary to overcome practical difficulties in training and setting examinations in the least developed countries.

(b)   There would also be many practical difficulties in developing a system of examinations and training which allows the candidates to attain a professional qualification that is of the same standard worldwide.

(c)   The second part of the project is to develop a certification system where institutions in developing countries could be certified to the effect that their qualification is equivalent to the benchmark. Currently, the ACCA scheme contains a certification component, but it certifies the equivalence of courses offered by educational institutions in developing countries with components of the ACCA programme. Once the project had been completed, the certification system would have to be implemented. There are precedents for the United Nations to become the certifying body, particularly the work of ICAO, IMO and IAEA. Their certifying schemes should be studied to see if they are relevant. Finally, there is the question of the funding of the certification system. It is unlikely that such a system would be self-financing since institutions in developing countries would not have the necessary resources to finance the review.

(d)   One should also assess how widely this qualification/certification system would be accepted. All recommendations made by ISAR are voluntary and not enforceable, and their implementation, either by governments or national professional bodies, is discretionary. If only a few countries asked for an "qualifications/certification" review, the benefits would not justify the costs of the project. If the accreditation earned by those countries were ignored during the recognition process, progress towards harmonization of requirements would be limited.

(e)   Lastly, this project is long-term in nature (a minimum of one to two years) and requires extra budgetary funds. It cannot be carried out on an ad hoc basis whereby ISAR members participate at the expense of their government, because not all governments may be able to afford the participation costs. For the project to be truly global in nature the ongoing participation of a wide selection of countries is essential.

There is no doubt that in theory the project is a worthwhile activity; however, because of its scale and implications, serious commitments must be undertaken to ensure that it is successful. In addition to financial resources, considerable political will must support the project to ensure its success.

IV. ISSUES OF IMPORTANCE TO DEVELOPING COUNTRIES

As previously mentioned, the WPPS has so far received information on the regulation of the accountancy profession from IFAC and on measures affecting the trade in accountancy services from OECD. This was supplemented by country questionnaires and by information from UNCTAD. This will be useful in its establishment of disciplines for education, technical standards and licensing.

The WPPS is to set guidelines for the recognition of qualifications. The measures for the different processes of recognition include harmonization, mutual recognition and autonomous recognition. Mutual recognition schemes work best in countries which have similar regulatory regimes and systems for obtaining a qualification. It is doubtful whether this system could work in countries with radically different regimes. Even in relatively homogeneous countries which have mutual recognition schemes, only a very small percentage of accountants have availed themselves of the process. So far, mutual recognition has not really reduced the barriers to trade in accountancy services even among developed countries. Added to this is the fact that mutual recognition procedures are also cumbersome, expensive and time-consuming to apply on a country-by-country basis. If all countries entered simultaneous negotiations, accounting qualifications would have to be examined in over 17,000 cases. Thus, the benefits of mutual recognition will be realized slowly.

In many developing countries accountancy is an emerging sector. In many cases it is underdeveloped and there are few qualified professionals. On the other hand, there is no shortage of professionals in most developed countries and some developing countries. UNCTAD studies attest that the service sector is a growth sector and as such is a source of jobs. The question is, who will qualify for these jobs? Accountancy services are skill-intensive rather than labour-resource- or capital-intensive. However, some developing countries have high-quality educational systems and can produce qualified accountants. Other developing countries will be unable to compete if qualification/recognition systems are more burdensome than necessary for ensuring the quality of service. Currently, there is a lack of demand for indigenous accountants and the important public engagements go to accountants working for the affiliates of international firms. This may explain why some developing countries have responded by limiting the number of foreign accountants allowed to practise in their countries. The difficult question is, how can developing countries extend access to foreign accountants in line with their own development needs? It should be borne in mind from the outset that the General Agreement on Trade in Services attempts to place all dealings on a more equal footing; Article IV contains an acknowledgement that special consideration should be given to countries which may not always be able to compete on an equal footing.

A balanced approach should be taken to qualification or skill requirements which recognizes the gap between the developed and developing countries. A benchmark could help here. When the WPPS exercise is completed, it will be difficult, but not impossible, for countries to maintain non-skill barriers. This might give accountants from developed countries easier access, while those from developing

countries might find it harder to have their credentials recognized. One way out of this dilemma is the harmonization route, which bases qualification requirements and recognition measures on multilaterally agreed criteria, as is suggested in Article VII of the GATS. The IFAC educational guidelines and the policy statement on the recognition of qualifications provide steps towards such criteria.
Nevertheless, the task of developing a benchmark for professional qualifications remains to be carried out if developing countries are to benefit from increased trade in accountancy services by upgrading credentials earned in their countries.

Notes

1   Communication from the OECD: "Work in the Area of Professional Services", S/WPPS/W/4, 14 November 1995, Add. 1 and 2.

2   "IFAC Questionnaire on Issues Related to International Trade in Accountancy Services: Summary of Responses", July 1995.

3   See, for example, *Accountancy Development in Africa: Challenge of the 1990s* (ST/CTC/109) and *International Accounting and Reporting Issues: 1993 Review* (UNCTAD/DTCI/3).

CHAPTER VI

REGULATION OF THE ACCOUNTANCY PROFESSION IN DEVELOPING COUNTRIES AND COUNTRIES IN TRANSITION

SUMMARY

The Working Party on Professional Services (WPPS) established by the World Trade Organization requested UNCTAD to provide information on various issues relating to regulation of the accountancy profession in 37 developing countries and countries in transition.

Information has been collected over the years through various questionnaires of the Intergovernmental Working Group of Experts on International Standards of Accounting and Reporting (ISAR). This information has been updated where possible by recontacting respondents, who were usually heads of professional accountancy bodies, government institutions and other regulatory or academic organizations. The update related to the following issues:

1. regulation of the accountancy profession in general, professional titles and professional bodies;
2. qualification and licensing requirements for individuals and firms;
3. possibilities for recognition of qualifications of foreign professionals;
4. technical standards and ethics.

Twenty-nine countries have responded so far. The results of this update and previous surveys have been tabulated to show as clearly as possible the situation in each country, and the objective of this report is to provide an overview of the results in the tables.

GENERAL CONCLUSIONS

I. Regulation of the accountancy profession

In more than half of the developing countries surveyed the activities of professional accountants and auditors are subject to government regulation, while in the remainder they are subject either to self-regulation by professional accountancy organizations, or to a combination of both government and professional self-regulation. There are also a few countries, approximately 10 per cent of those surveyed, particularly in Africa, where regulation of the profession is not yet organized.

The size of professional accountancy bodies and the scope of their activities, particularly the degree of their involvement in areas such as the development of national education and training programmes, formulation and control of licensing requirements and responsibility for standard-setting, vary considerably depending on local circumstances and the needs of the individual country. Some professional accountancy organizations are responsible for regulating all aspects of the profession, while others function merely as membership bodies through which members can communicate. It should be noted that often a self-regulatory professional accountancy organization is constituted by law and statutorily recognized as a regulatory and/or disciplinary body so that it has the necessary authority to carry out its functions and achieve its objectives, but it is actually controlled by its members and operated completely independently of government.

Recent updates from respondents indicated that in 40 per cent of the developing countries the profession is in its early stages of development; either there is no organized professional body or attempts are generally being made to establish an accounting profession, set up a statutorily recognized professional organization and develop requirements for individuals to obtain a professional title in order to provide accountancy services. A further 20 per cent of countries appear to have an accountancy profession in the middle stages of development, while 40 per cent have already established a relatively mature profession. Nevertheless, it is clear that the accountancy profession is still much less organized and regulated in some developing countries than in others, and that there is great disparity in the regulation of the accountancy profession not only between developing and developed countries, but also among the developing countries themselves.

In most countries in transition, particularly in the CIS, the profession is still heavily regulated by the government. The Ministry of Finance, the Audit Chamber and/ or Central Bank and Ministry of Justice are involved in the licensing and registration of professional accountants in public practice (i.e. independent auditors). Professional bodies are being created, such as the Association of Accountants and Auditors and the Union of Accountants. Their role so far has been to provide training and certificates to candidates so that they can obtain a licence.

II. Qualification and licensing requirements

In developing countries where the profession is already organized and regulated, individuals are normally required to meet certain conditions in order to qualify and obtain a professional title such as "chartered accountant" or "certified public accountant". In the majority of cases they have to undertake an educational programme, pass professional examinations and complete a period of approved practical training. Membership of a professional body is very often also required. In addition, there are normally requirements which have to be met before beginning professional education: an individual is usually required to have a university degree or at least to have reached university entrance level and successfully completed a prior course of professional education in specified subjects or passed an examination for admission to professional education. Prior payment of fees and registration with a professional body are sometimes required.

In some cases, individuals are required to complete the educational programme or sit the professional examinations of a professional body in another country, or even become a fully qualified member of an overseas body, in order to obtain a professional title, possibly where the size of the national body or country is such that it would not be economically feasible to establish a full national programme or where the profession is not yet fully developed. For example, professional bodies in five of the ten English-speaking African countries have a joint examination scheme arrangement with the Chartered Association of Certified Accountants in the United Kingdom and accountants in Namibia sit the examinations of the South African Institute of Chartered Accountants, while individuals in three English-speaking countries are required to obtain a professional qualification from an overseas body since there is no national qualification (although national requirements are currently being developed in Uganda). Only one country, The United Republic of Tanzania, currently has a full national scheme of examinations. Similarly, only three French-speaking African countries have developed full local examinations; in the remainder of such countries the profession is still relatively undeveloped and it is not possible to obtain a professional title unless one goes abroad to earn the title of "expert comptable" from the professional body in France, the Ordre des Experts Comptables et Comptables Agréés. Also, individuals in Cyprus obtain a professional qualification from an overseas body.

A period of practical experience of between two and five years, normally in an accounting or auditing environment, is required in virtually all countries. Approximately half the respondents indicated that this experience is required to be under the supervision of a member of the profession and/or in an approved practising firm to ensure the appropriate experience is acquired. However, in developing countries there are few accounting and auditing firms and so it is difficult to meet the practice requirement.

Apart from the above qualification requirements, there are often other conditions which have to be met in order for an individual to be licensed to practise. Membership of a professional body is almost always required before one can practise. Registration with a ministry or other institution is also often necessary. A few professional bodies, notably in Botswana and Malawi, require a period of post-qualification practical experience. Individual professionals are required to be licensed in order to practise in virtually all countries where the profession is regulated, other than in China, for example, where one cannot practise individually but must join a professional accounting firm.

On the other hand, professional accounting and auditing firms in developing countries are not always required to be licensed; in some 25 per cent of cases it is only the individuals themselves that are required to be licensed in order to practise. Licensing requirements for professional firms are quite varied and are detailed in the tables.

In the CIS the qualification requirements are stringent in that a university degree in a relevant field (i.e. accounting, economics, finance, taxation) is required or several years of special higher secondary education. In addition, specialized courses and examinations in Western accounting are being offered by the accounting associations. Also, five years of practical experience are required but not always under an appropriate person or firm. However, it is unrealistic to require this at the present time since there are so few licensed individuals or firms. Once this is completed, a certificate is obtained from certifying bodies and can be used to apply for a licence with the relevant regulatory body (the Audit Chamber, Ministry of Finance, Central Bank or insurance agency). Special designations are rather imprecise - "independent auditor", "licensed auditor" or, "certified auditor".

III. Recognition of foreign qualifications

It should be noted that the information received in relation to recognition of qualifications obtained by foreign professionals in another country was rather incomplete and the amount of detail provided varied considerably. However, on the basis of the information received, the following observations can been made.

Some countries, particularly in Africa, grant *automatic recognition* to individuals who are members of particular national professional accountancy bodies or hold an internationally recognized qualification considered to be equivalent to the national qualification (sometimes specified in the accounting law). In other instances, individuals may be granted recognition on an individual *case-by-case basis* if specifically authorized by the professional organization, ministry or other institution, usually after a review and validation of qualifications.

Other than *reciprocal agreements* for the recognition of qualifications between African countries in the same region and between Namibia and Australia and the United Kingdom, there do not appear to be any mutual recognition agreements in place.

Where foreign qualifications may be recognized, individuals are occasionally required to pass local taxation and law examinations to ensure they have adequate knowledge of local conditions. Membership of the local professional body or registration with the professional organization or ministry is often required. There is sometimes a residence and/or establishment requirement; in the Côte d'Ivoire there is a prior residence requirement of five years. Some countries also specify a period of practical experience before an individual can practise independently.

There are virtually no possibilities for the recognition of foreign qualifications in the CIS, although foreign accountants are allowed to obtain licences under the same conditions as national accountants. In some countries citizenship is required. Others, however, others require neither citizenship nor residence. In some countries the managing partner of foreign firms must have a national licence for the firm to be licensed to practise.

IV. Technical standards and ethics

Most countries have developed or are in the process of developing national accounting and auditing standards. More than 80 per cent of countries have a standard-setting committee of the professional organization or a specific government council established for this purpose, although some 15 pe rcent of these bodies are not operating at the present time. In some cases, international standards are adopted as the national standards, especially where the size of the accountancy profession is such that it would not be economically feasible to establish national standards. Monitoring the implementation of these standards is generally not very well organized, although in developing countries and, even where there is a body responsible for monitoring compliance with standards, some countries reported that the monitoring was ineffective or inadequate.

The results of the recent survey and of work carried out by Professor C. W. Nobes in the area of international accounting standards indicate similarities between various groups of countries and their use of international accounting standards. Countries with historical ties with, and strongly influenced by, the United Kingdom tend to have national rules which comply or mostly comply with international standards, or have less detailed rules which generally allow international standards to be followed. Conversely, the national rules of some of the French-speaking African countries tend not to conform with international standards but instead are based on the *plan comptable* (accounting plan) because of the existence of French influence. Nevertheless, most countries reported at least some use of international accounting standards, for example in the group accounts of listed companies.

Almost two-thirds of the countries surveyed have established or are in the process of developing a code of professional ethics, which is usually implemented by the professional accountancy bodies.

Accounting laws and auditing laws are being passed in many CIS countries. These are usually based on EC directives and international accounting and auditing standards. However, implementation is a long way off because the number of people needing retraining is very large. The absence of reliable Russian translations of international standards and the lack of suitable explanations or commentaries also make these standards difficult to use in national standard-setting.

V. Comparison of the situation in developing countries and countries in transition with that in developed countries

Following a review of the IFAC and OECD reports analysing the situation in developed countries, certain observations can be made. Where the accountancy profession is organized and regulated in developing countries and countries in transition, this regulation is generally effected by the government. The general structure of the profession and the conditions for qualification and licensing are often not dissimilar to those in developed countries, although the professions are sometimes not quite so developed in that, for example, they have not yet developed their own system of national examinations or supervisory procedures are not particularly advanced. There are a number of developing countries, however, where the profession is still to be organized and where students currently have to go overseas in order to obtain a professional qualification. Moreover, opportunities for the recognition of foreign qualifications tend to be much less common in developing countries and countries in transition. In developing guidelines for the recognition of foreign qualifications, WTO should bear in mind that many developing countries are starting at ground zero; therefore, the system for recognition should not be too burdensome.

In general, the developing countries and countries in transition seem to be moving in the direction of the profession in the developed countries. However, in many cases there is a long way to go and much technical assistance will be required, which is often not forthcoming or is ineffective. This would make it difficult for these countries to benefit fully from reductions in the barriers to trade in accountancy services. Thus, the development of a benchmark for professional qualifications might facilitate the strengthening of the professions in those countries and improve the preception of them. It would also cut the time and cost involved in evaluating developing country qualifications.

Table I.1. Regulation of the accountancy profession

Country	Regulation of accountancy profession			Body responsible for implementing regulation
	By law	Professional self-regulation	Combination of both	
Bangladesh		X		Institute of Chartered Accountants of Bangladesh Institute of Cost and Management Accountants of Bangladesh
Benin				(1)
Botswana		X		Botswana Institute of Accountants
Burkina Faso				(2)
Cameroon				(1)
Central African Republic				(1)
Chile	X			Superintendencia de Valores y Seguros (Securities and Exchange Commission)
China	X			China Institute of Certified Public Accountants Ministry of Finance
Côte d'Ivoire		X		Ordre des Experts Comptables et Comptables Agréés
Cyprus		X		Institute of Certified Public Accountants of Cyprus (3)
Czech Republic			X	Ministry of Finance (accounting) Chamber of Auditors of the Czech Republic (auditing)
Estonia	X			Ministry of Finance
Gabon	X			(2)
Guinea				(1)
India		X		Institute of Chartered Accountants of India Institute of Cost and Works Accountants of India

Table I.1 (cont.)

Country	Regulation of accountancy profession			Body responsible for implementing regulation
	By law	Professional self-regulation	Combination of both	
Israel	X			Auditors' Council (some aspects also supervised by Institute of Certified Public Accountants)
Lesotho		X		Lesotho Institute of Accountants
Madagascar			X	Ordre des Experts Comptables et Financiers et des Comptables Agréés de Madagascar Ministry of Finance, Ministry of Justice
Malawi	X			Society of Accountants in Malawi Malawi Accountants Board Public Accountants and Examinations Council
Mali			X	Ordre des Comptables Agréés et Experts Comptables du Mali Ministry of Finance, Conseil National de la Comptabilité
Mauritania		X		Ordre National des Experts Comptables Mauritaniens Disciplinary Committee and Registration Board under Ministry of Finance
Mauritius			X	Ministry of Finance, Mauritius Accounting and Auditing Standards Committee (standards) UK accountancy bodies (ICAEW, ACCA, CIMA) (other)
Morocco	X			Ordre des Experts Comptables Ministry of Finance, Ministry of Commerce and Industry
Mozambique	X			Ministry of Finance
Namibia		X		Institute of Chartered Accountants of Namibia Public Accountants and Auditors Board (Namibia) Public Accountants and Auditors Board of South Africa
Pakistan		X		Institute of Chartered Accountants of Pakistan Institute of Cost and Management Accountants of Pakistan

Table I.1 (cont.)

Country	Regulation of accountancy profession			Body responsible for implementing regulation
	By law	Professional self-regulation	Combination of both	
Peru		X		Colegio de Contadores Publicos (Association of Public Accountants)
Russian Federation	X			Ministry of Finance/Central Bank/Insurance Agency
Senegal	X			Ordre National des Experts et Evaluateurs Agréés du Sénégal Ministry of Justice
Sierra Leone		X		Institute of Chartered Accountants of Sierra Leone
Togo				(2)
Tunisia			X	Ordre des Experts Comptables de Tunisie Finance Ministry, Education Ministry
Uganda			X	Institute of Certified Public Accountants of Uganda (4)
Ukraine	X			Chamber of Auditors, Ministry of Finance, National Bank of Ukraine
United Rep. of Tanzania	X			National Board of Accountants and Auditors
Uzbekistan	X			Chamber of Auditors, Ministry of Finance (5)
Zambia		X		Zambia Institute of Certified Accountants
Total	13	12	6	

(1) Information unavailable.
(2) Regulation of accountancy profession not yet organized.
(3) Draft legislation awaits approval (expected in 1996), it governs regulation of all aspects of the accountancy profession and provides for the establishment of a new Council to be responsible for regulatory and disciplinary matters.
(4) Not yet fully operational; law passed in 1992 (Accountants Statute 1992).
(5) Once the new law is adopted (expected in 1996), regulation will be implemented by the newly created Accounting Standards Committee and by public professional associations.

Table I.2. Professional titles

Country	Professional titles	Body responsible for granting professional title	Government institution
Bangladesh	Chartered Accountant Cost and Management Accountant [not authorized to practise as public accountant unless specifically appointed by the Government]	Institute of Chartered Accountants of Bangladesh Institute of Cost and Management Accountants of Bangladesh	No No
Benin	(1)		
Botswana	Certified Public Accountant	Botswana Institute of Accountants	No
Burkina Faso	Expert Comptable Commissaire aux Comptes [statutory auditor]	Ordre des Experts Comptables et Comptables Agréés (France) Compagnie Nationale des Commissaires aux Comptes (France)	No No
Cameroon	(1)		
Central African Republic	(1)		
Chile	Public Accountant Auditor Accountant	Association of Accountants of Chile Association of Accountants of Chile	(1) (1)
China	Certified Public Accountant	Association of Accountants of Chile	Yes
Côte d'Ivoire	Expert Comptable Comptable Agréé [not authorized to audit]	Ordre des Experts Comptables et Comptables Agréés (France) Ordre des Experts Comptables et Comptables Agréés (France)	No No
Cyprus	Certified Public Accountant (Cyprus) In practice, accountants use titles granted by their respective overseas bodies	Institute of Certified Public Accountants of Cyprus Overseas bodies, e.g., ACCA, ICAEW	No
Czech Republic	Auditor [statutory auditor]	Chamber of Auditors of the Czech Republic	No
Estonia	Authorized Public Accountant/Authorized Independent Auditor	Estonian Auditing Board	Yes
Gabon	Expert Comptable Commissaire aux Comptes [statutory auditor]	Ordre des Experts Comptables et Comptables Agréés (France) Compagnie Nationale des Commissaires aux Comptes (France)	No No
Guinea	(1)		

Table I.2 (cont.)

Country	Professional titles	Body responsible for granting professional title	Government institution
India	Chartered Accountant	Institute of Chartered Accountants of India	No
	Cost and Works Accountant	Institute of Cost and Works Accountants of India	No
Israel	Certified Public Accountant	Auditors' Council under auspices of Ministry of Justice	Yes
Lesotho	Chartered Accountant	Lesotho Institute of Accountants	No
Madagascar	Expert Comptable et Financier	Ministries of Finance, Justice and Education	Yes
	Comptable Agréé [not authorized to audit]	Ministries of Finance, Justice and Education	Yes
Malawi	Certified Public Accountant	Malawi Accountants Board	Yes
Mali	Expert Comptable Agréé	Ordre des Experts Comptables et Comptables Agréés (France)	No
	Comptable Agréé [not authorized to audit]	Ordre des Experts Comptables et Comptables Agréés (France)	No
Mauritania	Expert Comptable	Registration Board under Ministry of Finance	Yes
	Commissaire aux Comptes [statutory auditor]	Registration Board under Ministry of Finance	Yes
Mauritius	Accountants use titles granted by their respective UK bodies	UK accountancy bodies (ACCA, ICAEW, CIMA)	No
Morocco	Expert Comptable	Ordre des Experts Comptables	No
	Comptable Agréé [not authorized to audit]	Commission headed by Minister of Finance	Yes
Mozambique	(1)		
Namibia	Chartered Accountant (Namibia)	Public Accountants and Auditors Board (Namibia)	No
Pakistan	Chartered Accountant	Institute of Chartered Accountants of Pakistan	(1)
	Cost and Management Accountant [authorized to audit private but not public companies]	Institute of Cost and Management Accountants of Pakistan	(1)
Peru	Public Accountant	Universities	No
	Chartered Public Accountant	Association of Public Accountants	No
	Independent Auditor	Association of Public Accountants	No
Russian Federation	Certified Professional Accountant	Ministry of Finance/Central Bank	Yes
	Certified Professional Auditor	Ministry of Finance/Central Bank	Yes

Table I.2 (cont.)

Country	Professional titles	Body responsible for granting professional title	Government institution
Senegal	Expert Comptable Agréé	Ordre des Experts Comptables et Comptables Agréés (France)	No
Sierra Leone	Chartered Accountant (Sierra Leone)	Institute of Chartered Accountants of Sierra Leone	No
Togo	Expert Comptable Commissaire aux Comptes [statutory auditor]	Ordre des Experts Comptables et Comptables Agréés (France) Compagnie Nationale des Commissaires aux Comptes (France)	No No
Tunisia	Expert Comptable Commissaire aux Comptes/Réviseur Légal [statutory auditor]	Ordre des Experts Comptables de Tunisie Ordre des Experts Comptables de Tunisie	No No
Uganda	Accountants use titles granted by their respective overseas bodies (3)	Overseas bodies (UK, US, Kenya, United Repulic of Tanzania)	
Ukraine	Chief Accountant	Various educational establishments	No
	Auditor	Chamber of Auditors	Yes
United Rep. of Tanzania	Certified Public Accountant Certified Public Accountant in Public Practice	National Board of Accountants and Auditors CPA in industry and commerce National Board of Accountants and Auditors	Yes (2) Yes (2)
Uzbekistan	Chief Accountant [accountant in commerce/industry] Licensed Auditor	Various educational establishments Ministry of Finance	No Yes
Zambia	Certified Accountant	Zambia Institute of Certified Accountants	No

(1) Information unavailable.
(2) Semi-government body, 40 per cent financed by government.
(3) Institute of Certified Public Accountants of Uganda and National Examinations Board still in the development stage; they are not expected to be fully operational.

Table I.3. Professional accountancy bodies

Country	Professional bodies	Statutorily recognized	Number of members 1996	Percentage of members working in each economic sector				
				Public practice	Industry/ Commerce	Government	Education	Retired/ Unemployed
Bangladesh	Institute of Chartered Accountants of Bangladesh (ICAB)	Yes	648	35	56	8	1	0
	Institute of Cost and Management Accountants of Bangladesh (ICMAB)	Yes	412	4	86	4	6	0
Benin	Compagnie d'Experts et Commissaires de Sociétés du Bénin (CECSB)	---	---	---	---	---	---	---
Botswana	Botswana Institute of Accountants (BIA)	Yes	403	29	67	2	2	0
Burkina Faso	Association des Experts Comptables et Comptables Agréés (1)	No	---	---	---	---	---	---
Cameroon	Ordre des Experts Comptables et Comptables Agréés (OECCA)	Yes	---	---	---	---	---	---
Central African Republic	---	---	---	---	---	---	---	---
Chile	Colegio de Contadores de Chile (Association of Accountants of Chile)	---	---	---	---	---	---	---
	Instituto de Contadores Profesionales Auditores (Institute of Accountants and Public Auditors)	---	---	---	---	---	---	---
China	China Institute of Certified Public Accountants (CICPA)	Yes	126 000	79	10	8	2	1
	Accounting Society of China (ASC)	No	---	---	---	---	---	---
Côte d'Ivoire	Ordre des Experts Comptables et Comptables Agréés (OECCA)	Yes	---	---	---	---	---	---
Cyprus	Institute of Certified Public Accountants of Cyprus (ICPAC)	No	741	77	9	11	1	2
Czech Republic	Chamber of Auditors of the Czech Republic	Yes	1 200	---	---	---	---	---
	Union of Accountants (2)	No	(2)10 000	---	---	---	---	---
Estonia	Estonian Auditing Board	---	---	---	---	---	---	---
Gabon	None (3)							
Guinea	Ordre des Experts Comptables et Comptables Agréés (OECCA)	---	---	---	---	---	---	---
India	Institute of Chartered Accountants of India (ICAI)	Yes	---	---	---	---	---	---
	Institute of Cost and Works Accountants of India (ICWAI)	Yes	---	---	---	---	---	---

Table I.3 (cont.)

Country	Professional bodies	Statutorily recognized	Number of members 1996	Percentage of members working in each economic sector				
				Public practice	Industry/ Commerce	Government	Education	Retired/ Unemployed
Israel	Institute of Certified Public Accountants (ICPA) (4)	No	approx. 7 000	35-40	60-65	0		
Lesotho	Lesotho Institute of Accountants (LIA)	Yes	140	28	72	0		
Madagascar	Ordre des Experts Comptables et Financiers et des Comptables Agréés de Madagascar (OECCAM)	Yes	42	95	5	0	0	0
Malawi	Society of Accountants in Malawi (SOCAM)	Yes	125	18	76	3	3	0
	Malawi Accountants Board (MAB)	Yes	---	---	---	---	---	---
	Public Accountants and Examinations Council (PAEC)	Yes	---	---	---	---	---	---
Mali	Ordre des Comptables Agréés et Experts Comptables du Mali (OCAECM)	Yes	23	100	0	0	0	0
	Association des Comptables du Mali (ACM)	No	22	100	0	0	0	0
Mauritania	Ordre National des Experts Comptables Mauritaniens (ONECM)	Yes	32	---	---	---	---	---
	Association des Comptables de Mauritanie (ASCOMA)	No	approx. 50	---	---	---	---	---
Mauritius	Association of Accountants in Mauritius (AAM) (1938)	No	(8)	---	---	---	---	---
	Chartered Association of Certified Accountants (ACCA Mauritius Branch) (1980)	No	(8)	---	---	---	---	---
	Society of Chartered Accountants	No	(8)	---	---	---	---	---
	Joint Accounting Council	No	(8)	---	---	---	---	---
Morocco	Ordre des Experts Comptables (OEC)	Yes	200	0	0	0	0	0
	Compagnie des Experts Comptables du Maroc	No	approx. 100	---	---	---	---	---
	Association Marocaine des Experts Comptables	No	approx. 40	---	---	---	---	---
Mozambique	---	---	---	---	---	---	---	---
Namibia	Institute of Chartered Accountants of Namibia (ICAN)	Yes	97	51	47	0	2	0
	Public Accountants and Auditors Board (Namibia) (PAAB (Namibia))	Yes	117	42	43	0	0	15 (5)
Pakistan	Institute of Chartered Accountants of Pakistan (ICAP)	Yes	1 919	23	77	0	0	0
	Institute of Cost and Management Accountants of Pakistan (ICMAP)	Yes	1 892	1	99	0	0	0
Peru	Colegio de Contadores Publicos (Association of Public Accountants)	Yes	14 555	---	---	---	---	---

Table I.3 (cont.)

Country	Professional bodies	Statutorily recognized	Number of members 1996	Percentage of members working in each economic sector				
				Public practice	Industry/ Commerce	Government	Education	Retired/ Unemployed
Russian Federation	Association of Accountants and Auditors of the Commonwealth	No	1 000	95	5	0	0	0
	Association of Accountants and Auditors of Russia	No	800	98	2	0	0	0
	Chamber of Auditors of Russia	No	28	100	0	0	0	0
	Institute of Professional Accountants (6)	No	--	--	--	--	--	--
Senegal	Ordre National des Experts et Evaluateurs Agréés du Sénégal (ONEEAS)	Yes	60	100	0	0	0	0
	Association des Comptables Professionels du Sénégal (ACPS)	No	--	--	--	--	--	--
Sierra Leone	Institute of Chartered Accountants of Sierra Leone (ICASL)	Yes	58	50	33	5	3	9
Togo	Association Togolaise des Professeurs de Comptabilité (ATPC)	No	30	--	--	--	--	--
	Comite National de SYSCOA (CNS)	--	20	--	--	--	--	--
Tunisia	Ordre des Experts Comptables de Tunisie (OECT)	Yes	170	84	5	1	10	0
Uganda	Institute of Certified Public Accountants of Uganda (ICPAU) (1992)(7)	Yes	98	60	30	8	0	0
	Certified Accountants Society of Uganda (ACCA Uganda Branch) (1978)	No	approx. 60	--	--	--	--	--
Ukraine	Association of Accountants of Ukraine	No	1 000-2 000	0	100	0	0	0
	Union of Auditors of Ukraine	No	1 000	100	0	0	0	0
	Chamber of Auditors of Ukraine	No	--	--	--	--	--	--
United Republic of Tanzania	National Board of Accountants and Auditors (NBAA)	Yes	935	30	70	0	0	0
	Tanzania Association of Accountants (TAA)	No	576	19	77	2	2	0
Uzbekistan	Association of Accountants and Auditors	No	600	98	0	0	2	0
Zambia	Zambia Institute of Certified Accountants (ZICA)	Yes	301	36	59	1	4	0

-- = Information unavailable.

(1) A professional body of Experts Comptables et Commissaires aux Comptes is in the process of being created.
(2) Not all members are professional accountants.
(3) A professional body of Experts Comptables is in the process of being created; there are currently approximately 10 fully qualified accountants in Gabon.
(4) 95 per cent of licensed accountants in Israel are members of ICPA.
(5) 15 per cent are non-resident.
(6) To be created
(7) Not yet fully operational.
(8) There are currently approximately 200 qualified accountants engaged in public practice in Mauritius.

Table II.1. Qualification requirements

Country	Title	Requirements to acquire professional title					
		Educational qualification	Years of education	Years of practice and with whom	Professional examination	Membership in professional body	Other
Bangladesh	Chartered accountant	Second class graduate or holder of Master's degree	3 to 3 1/2 years	3 to 3 1/2 years in firm of chartered accountants (depending on educational qualifications)	Intermediate and final	Yes - ICAB	
	Cost and management accountant	Any university degree	2 1/2 years	None required	Intermediate and final	Yes - ICMAB	
Benin	(6)						
Botswana	Certified Public Accountant	Recognized university degree or equivalent, or secondary education + AAT qualification		3 or 4 years under supervision in firm of Certified Public Accountants (depending on qualification)	Yes (2) (4) ACCA taxation, law public sector financial management papers replaced by local variant papers	Yes - BIA and either ACCA (UK) or other professional body of accountants recognized by BIA	
Burkina Faso	Expert Comptable, Commissaire aux Comptes	University degree; Diplôme d'Expertise Comptable	Baccalauréat + 7 years (abroad)	3 years' supervised practice (abroad)	Yes (abroad)	Voluntary	Note: Only a limited number of professionals have the French Diplôme d'Expertise Comptable; there is no regulation other than in the banking sector) regarding qualifications required for use of titles
Cameroon	(6)						
Central African Republic	(6)						
Chile	Public Accountant	University degree	5 years	6 months' accounting experience	Yes		
	Auditor Accountant	University degree	5 years	3 years' auditing experience	Yes		

Table II.1 (cont.)

Country	Title	Educational qualification	Years of education	Years of practice and with whom	Professional examination	Membership in professional body	Other
				Requirements to acquire professional title			
China	Certified Public Accountant	University degree		3 years in accounting or auditing field for accountant; 2 years in accounting firm for statutory auditor	Yes	Yes - CICPA	Must join accounting firm, otherwise loses title of CPA immediately; cannot be government officer
Côte d'Ivoire	Expert Comptable, Comptable Agréé	French Diplôme d'Expertise Comptable or other diploma in accounting	8 to 10 years (abroad)	3 years' supervised practice (abroad)	Yes (abroad)	Yes - OECCA	
Cyprus	As per overseas accounting bodies (1)						
Czech Republic	Auditor	University degree in economics or law	4 to 5 years at university level	5 years, not necessarily under supervision of a member of the profession	Yes	Yes - Chamber of Auditors	Czech language
Estonia	Authorized Public Accountant	University degree	4 years' practice as company accountant or 2 1/2 years' practice as assistant in an audit firm	Yes			
Gabon	Expert Comptable, Commissaire aux Comptes	University degree; Diplôme d'Expertise comptable (abroad)	Baccalauréat + 7 years (abroad)	3 years (abroad)	Yes (abroad)		
Guinea	(6)						
India	Chartered Accountant		University degree; training with practising Chartered Accountant	3 years' practical experience	Intermediate and final	Yes - ICAI	
	Cost and Works Accountant	Secondary school or university degree	3 years	3 years	Yes	Yes - ICWAI	

(Table II.1. cont'd)

Country	Title	Requirements to acquire professional title					
		Educational qualification	Years of education	Years of practice and with whom	Professional examination	Membership in professional body	Other
Israel	Certified Public Accountant	University degree not necessary, but very few students do not have university degree		2 years, in auditing and monitored by "supervising CPA" authorized by Council of Auditors, usually in CPA practice	Yes		
Lesotho	Chartered Accountant	University degree	4 1/2 years after obtaining degree	Not required	Yes (2)	Yes - LIA	
Madagascar	Expert Comptable et Financier	University degree	Baccalauréat + 4 to 5 years	3 years in firm of Experts Comptables, or 2 years in firm of Experts Comptables and 1 year in accounting elsewhere	Yes (5)	No	
	Comptable Agréé	University degree	Baccalauréat + 2 years	2 years in firm of Expert Comptables	Yes (5)	No	
Malawi	Certified Public Accountant	University degree or secondary education + AAT qualification		500 days' experience under registered training contract with member of SOCAM in any accounting environment	Yes (2) Local examination level 1 + ACCA examinations levels 2 & 3 (taxation and law replaced by local variant papers)	Yes - SOCAM	
Mali	Expert Comptable Agréé	French Diplôme d'Expertise Comptable (abroad)	Baccalauréat + 7 years	3 years	Yes		
	Comptable Agréé	French Diplôme d'Expertise Comptable or equivalent (abroad)	Baccalauréat + 5 years	3 years	Yes		
Mauritania	Expert Comptable, Commissaire aux Comptes	French Diplôme d'Expertise Comptable	Baccalauréat + 7 years	3 years	Yes	Yes - ONECM	

Table II.1 (cont.)

Country	Title	Requirements to acquire professional title					
		Educational qualification	Years of education	Years of practice and with whom	Professional examination	Membership in professional body	Other
Mauritius	As per UK accounting bodies						
Morocco	Expert Comptable	University degree	3 years	3 years in firm of Experts Comptables	Yes	Yes - OEC	
	Comptable Agréé	University degree		5 years; not in firm of Experts Comptables	No	No	
Mozambique	(6)						
Namibia	Chartered Accountant (Namibia)	Honours degree		3 years (graduate) or 5 years (studying for degree part-time), mostly in firms of chartered accountants)	Final qualifying examination of PAAB of South Africa	Yes - PAAB (Namibia)	
Pakistan	Chartered Accountant	University degree or foundation course of ICAP	4 to 5 years (depending on educational qualification)	Yes - 4 to 5 years	Yes - ICAP		
	Cost and Management Accountant	University degree	3 years	Yes - 3 years	Yes - ICMAP		
Peru	Public Accountant	Bachelors' degree in accountancy	5 years	Not required	Yes	No	
	Chartered Public Accountant	Must be Public Accountant	Not required	No	Yes - APA		
	Independent Auditor	Must be Chartered Public Accountant		3 years as accountant or auditor	No	Yes - APA	

Table II.1 (cont.)

Country	Title	Requirements to acquire professional title				Membership in professional body	Other
		Educational qualification	Years of education	Years of practice and with whom	Professional examination		
Russian Federation	Chief Accountant	Specialized secondary school or university degree					
	Certified Auditor	Specialized secondary school or university degree in law/economics	5 years	At least 3 years' continuous practical experience in the previous 5 years	Yes	No	
Senegal	Expert Comptable Agréé	University degree; Diplôme d'Expertise Comptable (abroad)	4 years (abroad)	3 years (abroad)	Yes (abroad)		Note: Only a limited number of professionals have the French Diplôme d'Expertise Comptable; some individuals acquire the right to practise as professionals even though they do not meet French qualification requirements
Sierra Leone	Chartered Accountant (Sierra Leone)	University degree or AAT qualification	8 years	2 years with member or firm in public practice	Yes (2)	Yes - ICASL	
Togo	Expert Comptable	University degree; Diplôme d'Expertise Comptable (abroad)	Baccalauréat + 7 years (abroad)	3 years in firm of Experts Comptables (abroad)	Yes (abroad)	Yes - OECCA (France)	
	Commissaire aux Comptes	University degree; Diplôme d'Expertise Comptable or equivalent (abroad)	Baccalauréat + 5 years (abroad)	3 years in audit firm (abroad)	Yes (abroad)	Yes - CNCC (France)	
Tunisia	Expert Comptable, Commissaire aux Comptes/Réviséur Légal	Diploma	7 years after baccalauréat/secondary school	3 years in firm of Experts Comptables, or 1 year in a company and 2 years in firm of Experts Comptables	Yes	Yes - OECT	

Table II.1 (cont.)

Country	Title	Requirements to acquire professional title					
		Educational qualification	Years of education	Years of practice and with whom	Professional examination	Membership in professional body	Other
Uganda	As per overseas accounting bodies (1)						
Ukraine	Chief Accountant Certified Auditor	University degree University degree		At least 2 years' practice At least 3 years' practice	Yes	No	
United Republic of Tanzania	Certified Public Accountant	B.Com or Advanced Diploma in Accountancy	16 years; 4 years at university level	3 years under supervision of qualified member	Yes - CPA levels I-IV	Yes - NBAA & TAA	
	Certified Public Accountant in Public Practice	B.Com or Advanced Diploma in Accountancy	16 years; 4 years at unversity level	3 years under supervision of statutory auditor	Yes - CPA levels I-IV	Yes - NBAA & TAA	
Uzbekistan	Chief Accountant	Specialized secondary school and/or higher education	5 years	At least 3 months	Yes	No	
	Certified Auditor	University degree	5 years	5 years as accountant, economist or auditor	Yes	Yes	Registration with Ministry of Justice and Ministry of Finance
Zambia	Certified Accountant	University degree	4 to 6 years	3 years' approved accounting experience	Yes (2) (3) (4)	Yes - ZICA	

(1) National requirements being developed.
(2) Joint examination scheme agreement with ACCA (UK).
(3) Students may also study for qualification from ICAEW (UK); not a joint scheme agreement.
(4) Students may also study for qualification from CIMA (UK); not a joint scheme agreement.
(5) Final examinations currently being developed.
(6) Information unavailable.

Table II.2. Additional licensing requirements for individuals

Country	Additional requirements to acquire licence							Other	Body responsible for granting licence
	Membership in professional body	Registration with ministry/ institution	Indemnity insurance	Oath	No criminal record	Police inquiry	Minimum age		
Bangladesh	X	X			X		X (CA)	2 years' post-qualification training	Institute of Chartered Accountants of Bangladesh for statutory auditors/management consultants; Institute of Cost and Management Accountants of Bangladesh for cost and management consultants (not authorized to act as public accountants/statutory auditors)
Benin	(1)								
Botswana	X		X		X			Not bankrupt or of unsound mind, or company registered under Companies Act; must be resident and hold practising certificate (requires membership of BIA for at least 2 years, and 12 months' post-qualification experience under supervision in firm of CPAs)	Botswana Institute of Accountants
Burkina Faso		X		X	X	X	X	These requirements are for those Commissaire aux Comptes who wish to register with the Court of Appeal; otherwise no specific authorization is required to practise	Court of Appeal
Cameroon	(1)								
Central African Republic	(1)								
Chile		X			X		X		Securities and Exchange Commission
China	X	X			X			Must be a member of a CPA firm; cannot practise independently	
Côte d'Ivoire	X	X	X	X	X	X	X		Registration Board of Ordre des Experts Comptables et Comptables Agréés
Cyprus	X							No licensing requirements as such at present (2); but to audit a public company must be member of a UK professional body	
Czech Republic	X		X		X			Czech citizenship	Chamber of Auditors of the Czech Republic

Table II.2 (cont.)

Country	Membership in professional body	Registration with ministry/ institution	Indemnity insurance	Oath	No criminal record	Police inquiry	Minimum age	Other	Body responsible for granting licence
			Additional requirements to acquire licence						
Estonia		X			X				(1)
Gabon		X			X				Ministry of Trade and Industry
Guinea	(1)								
India	(1)								
Israel		X					X		Auditors' Council
Lesotho	X							5 years' practical experience with a practising firm or other responsible position	Lesotho Institute of Accountants
Madagascar	X		(3)	X	X	X	X	Madagascar nationality (3)	Ordre des Experts Comptables et Financiers et des Comptables Agréés de Madagascar
Malawi	X							30 months' post-qualification experience in office of practising accountant	Society of Accountants in Malawi
Mali	X	X					X		Conseil National de la Comptabilité
Mauritania	X	X	X	X	X	X	X	Mauritanian nationality or reciprocal agreement with country of applicant	National Registration Board of Ordre National des Experts Comptables Mauritaniens
Mauritius	X							Any other licensing requirements of respective UK accounting bodies	Minister of Finance or UK accountancy bodies (by delegation from the Minister of Finance)
Morocco	X		X		X	X	X	Moroccan nationality or reciprocal agreement with country of applicant	Ordre des Experts Comptables
Mozambique	(1)								
Namibia	X				X			Not insolvent	Public Accountants and Auditors Board (Namibia)
Pakistan	X				X		X		Institute of Chartered Accountants of Pakistan for Chartered Accountants; Institute of Cost and Management Accountants of Pakistan for Cost and Management Accountants

Table II.2 (cont.)

Country	Additional requirements to acquire licence								Body responsible for granting licence
	Membership in professional body	Registration with ministry/ institution	Indemnity insurance	Oath	No criminal record	Police inquiry	Minimum age	Other	
Peru	X	X		X				Fulfilment of requirements for independent auditor	Association of Public Acountants
Russian Federation		X			X			Citizenship	Ministry of Finance, Central Bank, Insurance Agency
Senegal	X	X	X	X	X	X	X	Citizenship	Ordre National des Experts et Evaluateurs Agréés du Sénégal
Sierra Leone	X								Institute of Chartered Accountants of Sierra Leone
Togo		X			X	X		Acceptance by Ministry of Education and Finance of Commissaires aux Comptes	Ministry of Trade and Commerce
Tunisia	X			X	X			Tunisian citizenship	Ordre des Experts Comptables de Tunisie
Uganda	X	X						Licensing requirements of respective overseas accounting bodies (2)	Council of Institute of Certified Public Accountants of Uganda
Ukraine								Citizenship	Chamber of Auditors
United Republic of Tanzania	X							Practising certificate, granted after examination passed and 2 years' practical experience completed	Registrar of Business Names on receipt of clearance certificate from NBAA
Uzbekistan	X	X			X			Citizenship, residence; audit licences issued after registration with Ministry of Finance and Ministry of Justice	Ministry of Finance
Zambia	X	X			X			Auditors are required to have 30 months' practical experience with an approved auditing firm (this can be part of the initial 3 years' qualifying experience, provided it is with an approved auditing firm)	Zambia Institute of Certified Accountants
Total	23	17	6	7	20	7	11		

(1) Information unavailable.
(2) National requirements being developed.
(3) Currently under consideration.

Table II.3. Licensing requirements for professional accounting/auditing firms

Country	Professional firms required to be licensed	Additional requirements which must be met	Body responsible for granting licence
Bangladesh	Yes	Minimum standard of office, clients, library, etc.	Institute of Chartered Accountants of Bangladesh for statutory auditors/management consultants; Institute of Cost and Management Accountants of Bangladesh for cost and management consultants
Benin	(3)		
Botswana	No	Only individuals themselves are required to hold practising certificates; however, a firm cannot describe itself as "Certified Public Accountants" unless all members hold BIA practising certificates	
Burkina Faso	No	Commercial licence only required	
Cameroon	(3)		
Central African Republic	(3)		
Chile	Yes	50 per cent of share capital must be held by professional auditors Registration in Register of Auditors	Securities and Exchange Commission
China	Yes		China Institute of Certified Public Accountants
Côte d'Ivoire	Yes	Limited liability company (SARL): minimum capital 5,000,000 FCFA Incorporated comapny (SA): minimum capital 1,000,000 FCFA	Registration Board of Ordre des Experts Comptables et Comptables Agréés
Cyprus	No(1)		
Czech Republic	Yes	At least 60 per cent of equity or voting rights must belong to Czech statutory auditors	Chamber of Auditors of the Czech Republic
Estonia	No		
Gabon	Yes	Registration with the Ministry of Trade and Industry	Ministry of Trade and Industry
Guinea	(3)		

Table II.3 (cont.)

Country	Professional firms required to be licensed	Additional requirements which must be met	Body responsible for granting licence
India	(3)		
Israel	No		
Lesotho	No		
Madagascar	Yes	65 per cent of share capital must be held by Experts Comptables et Financiers	Ordre des Experts Comptables et Financiers et des Comptables Agréés de Madagascar
Malawi	Yes		Society of Accountants in Malawi
Mali	Yes	Partnerships must have at least 3 partners, of whom 2 are members of Ordre des Comptables Agréés et Experts Comptables du Mali	Conseil National de la Comptabilité
Mauritania	Yes	Registration with Ordre des Experts Comptables Mauritaniens (OECM) Shareholders must be members of OECM Only members of OECM may certify accounts	National Registration Board of Ordre National des Experts Comptables Mauritaniens
Mauritius	Yes	At least one member of the firm should be ordinarily resident in Mauritius	Minister of Finance or UK accountancy bodies and professionally qualified (by delegation from the Minister of Finance)
Morocco	Yes	At least 75 per cent of share capital held by Experts Comptables All partners must be Experts Comptables	Ordre des Experts Comptables
Mozambique	(3)		
Namibia	Yes	Registration with Public Accountants and Auditors Board (Namibia) All partners must be Chartered Accountants	Public Accountants and Auditors Board (Namibia)
Pakistan	Yes	Registration of firm with ICAP/ICMAP All partners must obtain practising certificate from their respective institutes	Institute of Chartered Accountants of Pakistan or Institute of Cost and Management Accountants of Pakistan
Peru	No	Commercial licence only required from City Council	
Russian Federation	Yes	Registration with Ministry; no criminal record	Ministry of Finance, Central Bank, Insurance Agency

Table II.3 (cont.)

Country	Professional firms required to be licensed	Additional requirements which must be met	Body responsible for granting license
Senegal	Yes	At least 65 per cent of share capital held by professionals	Ordre National des Experts et Evaluateurs Agréés du Sénégal
Sierra Leone	No	Only the individuals themselves are required to hold practising certificates	Institute of Chartered Accountants of Sierra Leone
Togo	Yes		Ministry of Trade and Commerce
Tunisia	Yes	Registration of firm with Ordre des Experts Comptables de Tunisie Management must be exercised by individual members of Ordre des Experts Comptables Limited liability company (SARL): at least 75per cent of share capital must be held by Experts Comptables Incorporated company (SA): 100 per cent of share capital must be held by Experts Comptables	Ordre des Experts Comptables de Tunisie
Uganda	Yes	Registration with Institute of Certified Public Accountants of Uganda	Institute of Certified Public Accountants of Uganda
Ukraine	Yes	Company director must have certificate for audit firm to obtain licence	Chamber of Auditors
United Republic of Tanzania	Yes	Registration with National Board of Accountants and Auditors Professional indemnity insurance cover All partners must be Certified Public Accountants in Public Practice	Registrar of Business Names on receipt of clearance certificate from National Board of Accountants and Auditors
Uzbekistan	No (2)		
Zambia	Yes	All partners must hold practising certificates Use names of partners for name of firm Sole trader or partnership only permitted	Zambia Institute of Certified Accountants

(1) National requirement currently being developed.
(2) Once the new accounting law has been adopted (expected in 1996), professional firms will be required to be licensed; Ministry of Finance will be responsible for granting licences.
(3) Information unavailable.

Table II.4. Content of professional education

Country	Financial accounting	Cost accounting	Government accounting	Auditing	Taxation	International accounting standards	Professional ethics	Electronic data processing	General law	Economics	Other
Bangladesh	X	X	X	X	X	X	X	X	X	X	Management accounting Financial management Statistics
Benin	(2)										
Botswana	X	X		X	X	X	X	X	X	X	
Burkina Faso	As per French accounting body										
Cameroon	(2)										
Central African Republic	(2)										
Chile	X	X		X	X			X	X	X	
China	X	X	X	X	X	X	X	X	X		
Côte d'Ivoire	X	X	X	X	X	X	X	X	X	X	Company valuation Business management
Cyprus	As per overseas accounting bodies(1)										
Czech Republic	X	X	X	X	X	X	X	X	X	X	Company law Business management
Estonia	X	X	X								
Gabon	As per French accounting body										
Guinea	(2)										

Table II.4 (cont.)

Country	Financial accounting	Cost accounting	Government accounting	Auditing	Taxation	International accounting standards	Professional ethics	Electronic data processing	General law	Economics	Other
India	(2)										
Israel	X	X	X	X	X	X	X	X	X	X	
Lesotho	X	X		X	X	X		X	X	X	
Madagascar	X	X	X	X	X	X	X	X	X	X	
Malawi	X	X	X	X	X	X	X	X	X	X	
Mali	As per French accounting body										
Mauritania	X	X	X	X	X	X	X	X	X	X	Mathematics/statistics Foreign languages
Mauritius	X	X	X	X	X	X	X	X	X	X	Financial management Company law Management Qualitative techniques
Morocco	X	X	X	X	X	X	X	X	X	X	Mathematics/statistics
Mozambique	(2)										
Namibia	X	X		X	X	X	X	X	X	X	
Pakistan	X	X	X	X	X	X	X	X	X	X	
Peru	X	X	X	X	X	X	X	X	X	X	Management Communication skills Psychology/sociology Mathematics/statistics

Table II.4 (cont.)

Country	Subjects included in professional education										
	Financial accounting	Cost accounting	Government accounting	Auditing	Taxation	International accounting standards	Professional ethics	Electronic data processing	General law	Economics	Other
Russian Federation	X	X		X	X	X	X	X	X	X	
Senegal	X	X		X	X	X	X	X	X	X	
Sierra Leone	X	X		X	X	X	X	X	X	X	
Togo	As per French accounting body										
Tunisia	X	X		X	X	X		X	X	X	Mathematics/statistics Business management
Uganda	As per overseas accounting bodies (1)										
Ukraine	X	X	X	X	X	X	X	X	X	X	
United Republic of Tanzania	X	X	X	X	X	X		X	X	X	
Uzbekistan	X	X	X	X	X	X	X	X	X	X	
Zambia	X	X		X	X	X	X	X	X	X	Management Managerial finance

(1) National requirements currently being developed.
(2) Information unavailable.

Table III. Recognition of foreign qualifications

Country	Possibilities exist for recognition of qualifications obtained by foreign professionals in another country	Where foreign qualifications may be recognized — Method of recognition: Case-by-case basis	Automatic recognition	Mutual recognition	Full local examination required	Local training course required	Accreditation/licensing requirements imposed on foreign professionals
Bangladesh	Yes - members of ICAEW	X			No (2)	No	Membership in ICAB; residence; establishment of office
Benin	(3)						
Botswana	Yes - members of professional bodies which are members of IASC/IFAC (the majority of professional accountants in Botswana are foreign professionals)		X		Usually taxation and law	No	Residence; must also be member of BIA and hold BIA practising certificate to practise independently (includes additional requirement for foreign professionals to pass local taxation and law examinations)
Burkina Faso	Yes - accountants qualified in France		X		No	No	
Cameroon	(3)						
Central African Republic	(3)						
Chile	No						
China	No						
Côte d'Ivoire	Yes	X			No	No	Residence for at least 5 years in Côte d'Ivoire and continued professional experience; review of qualifications by OECCA
Cyprus	Yes - members of UK professional accountancy bodies (ICAEW, ACCA)		X		No (2)	No	(1)
	Other accountants holding similar qualifications	X			No (2)	No	Currently, recognition requires at least 3 years' practical experience in a professional accounting/ auditing firm and authority of the Council of Ministers (1)

Table III (cont.)

Country	Possibilities exist for recognition of qualifications obtained by foreign professionals in another country	Where foreign qualifications may be recognized					Accreditation/licensing requirements imposed on foreign professionals
		Method of recognition			Full local examination required	Local training course required	
		Case-by-case basis	Automatic recognition	Mutual recognition			
Czech Republic	Yes	X			Law		Knowledge of Czech language and laws required; also membership in Chamber of Auditors. May sign statutory audit report only if member of firm where 60 per cent of equity/voting rights are held by statutory auditors with Czech citizenship
Estonia	No						
Gabon	Yes - professional accountants qualified in France			X	No	No	Registration with Ministry of Trade and Industry
	Yes - professional accountants in Central Africa (reciprocal agreement of the Customs and Economic Union of Central Africa (UDEAC))			X	No	No	Registration with Ministry of Trade and Industry; authorization from UDEAC Management Board
Guinea	(3)						
India	Yes - members of certain professional bodies in Australia, Myanmar, Pakistan, South Africa, Sri Lanka, UK		X				Residence
Israel	No (other than certain rules and exemptions for individuals immigrating to Israel)						

(Table III (cont.)

Country	Possibilities exist for recognition of qualifications obtained by foreign professionals in another country	Method of recognition — Case-by-case basis	Method of recognition — Automatic recognition	Method of recognition — Mutual recognition	Full local examination required	Local training course required	Accreditation/licensing requirements imposed on foreign professionals
Lesotho	Yes - holders of certain recognized qualifications (as specified in Accountants Act 1977, amended by Accountants (Amendment) Act 1984)		X		No	No	Recognized qualification; membership in Lesotho Institute of Accountants; establishment in country
Madagascar	No						
Malawi	Yes - members of professional bodies which are members of IFAC		X		Usually taxation and law	No	Registration with MAB and SOCAM; to practise independently, required to have 30 months experience in practising firm in Malawi and pass local taxation and company law examinations
Mali	Yes - accountants qualified in France		X		No	No	Licence from CNC
Mauritania	Yes - accountants qualified in Algeria, Libya, Morocco and Tunisia		X		No	No	
	Yes - accountants with qualification equivalent to Frence Diplôme d'Expertise Comptable (however, no specific reciprocity agreements exist at present)				No	No	Reciprocity agreement required with country of applicant; 2 to 3 years' practical experience in local accounting firm
Mauritius	Members of UK accountancy bodies		X		No	No	Work permit; residence
	Chartered Accountants qualified in India and who are members of Institute of Chartered Accountants of India		X		No	No	Under the Mauritius Offshore Business Activities Act 1992, audit companies in the off-shore jurisdiction can be accredited/licensed

Table III (cont.)

Country	Possibilities exist for recognition of qualifications obtained by foreign professionals in another country	Where foreign qualifications may be recognized					Accreditation/licensing requirements imposed on foreign professionals
		Method of recognition			Full local examination required	Local training course required	
		Case-by-case basis	Automatic recognition	Mutual recognition			
Morocco	Yes - accountants qualified in Algeria, Libya, Mauritania and Tunisia		X		No	No	Residence
Mozambique	(3)						
Namibia	UK and Australian qualified accountants			X	Usually taxation and law	No	Registration with PAAB (Namibia); residence; establishment
	Members of PAAB (South Africa); accountants qualified in Zimbabwe			X	No	No	Registration with PAAB (Namibia)
Pakistan	Members of ICAEW		X		Corporate taxation and law	No	Membership of ICAP; must apply for practising certificate
	Members of CIMA (UK)		X		Law and EDP		
Peru	Yes	X			No	No	Validation of foreign qualification by a local accounting university faculty; registration in Association of Public Accountants; authentication of foreign certificates by individual's Foreign Affairs Ministry
Russian Federation	No						

Table III (cont.)

Country	Possibilities exist for recognition of qualifications obtained by foreign professionals in another country	Where foreign qualifications may be recognized					Accreditation/licensing requirements imposed on foreign professionals
		Method of recognition			Full local examination required	Local training course required	
		Case-by-case basis	Automatic recognition	Mutual recognition			
Sierra Leone	Yes - members of other professional bodies approved under regulations made by the Council as having status equivalent to that of ICASL		X		No	No	As detailed in Institute of Chartered Accountants of Sierra Leone Act 1988
Togo	Yes, but no specific agreements		X		No	No	Obtain licence for establishment of business
Tunisia	Yes - accountants qualified in Algeria, Libya, Mauritania and Morocco Other similarly qualified accountants holding qualification equivalent to the Tunisian "Expert Comptable" as agreed by Education Ministry (however, no specific reciprocity agreements exist at present)			X	No	No	Reciprocity agreement required with respective country; granted provisional registration with Ordre des Experts Comptables, followed by authorization of Ministries of Finance and Foreign Affairs
Uganda	Yes - holders of recognized overseas qualifications	X			No (1)	No (1)	Membership of ICPAU

Table III (cont.)

Country	Possibilities exist for recognition of qualifications obtained by foreign professionals in another country	Where foreign qualifications may be recognized					Accreditation/licensing requirements imposed on foreign professionals
		Method of recognition			Full local examination required	Local training course required	
		Case-by-case basis	Automatic recognition	Mutual recognition			
Ukraine	No						
United Republic of Tanzania	Yes - members of UK, US and Canadian accountancy bodies		X		No (2)	No	Registration with NBAA (given temporary registration)
	Other qualified accountants	X					Applications considered by NBAA
Uzbekistan	Foreign qualifications are not generally recognized	X			Yes	Yes - 3 months	5 years' practical experience; 3-month training course given by Association of Accountants and Auditors; full examination; residence; knowledge of language; licence registered with Ministries of Justice and Finance
Zambia	Yes - members of certain professional accounting bodies in UK, US, New Zealand, Australia, Canada and Zimbabwe (as specified in Statutory Instrument No. 40 of 1994)		X				Membership of recognized professional body (as indicated in Statutory Instrument No. 40 of 1994); 30 months' experience in practising firm; one year membership of ZICA

(1) National requirements being developed.
(2) Currently no examination, but consideration being given to developing requirement for foreign professionals to pass local taxation and law examinations in future.
(3) Information unavailable.

Table IV.1. National accounting and auditing standards

Country	Number of national accounting standards	Number of national auditing standards	Standard-setting body governing accounting and auditing	Compliance monitoring body	Other government laws and regulations
Bangladesh	16	15	Institute of Chartered Accountants of Bangladesh	Institute of Chartered Accountants of Bangladesh	Securities and Exchange Rules 1987; Tax Law; other government laws, e.g. banking and insurance laws
Benin	(7)	(7)	Conseil National de la Comptabilité (6)	Government Ministry in charge of overseeing operations of public companies	National Accounting Plan, Decree No. 88 - 005 of 1988 applicable to public companies; Commercial Law; Foreign Capital Investment Law; Banking Law
Botswana	IASs	ISAs	Botswana Institute of Accountants		International accounting and auditing standards adopted by BIA without modification; Companies Act
Burkina Faso	0.0	0.0	Conseil National de la Comptabilité (6)		General Accounting Plan based on Plan OCAM, Commercial Law; Business Corporation Law; Foreign Capital Investment Law; Accounting Act; Income Tax Law; accounting regulations relating to banks and financial institutions
Cameroon	(7)	(7)			General Accounting Plan, Company Law (French Law of 1867); Foreign Capital Investment Law; Income Tax Law; Banking Law
Central African Republic	(7)	(7)			
Chile	(3)	(3)	Association of Accountants of Chile (accounting standards); Association of Accountants and Public Auditors (auditors' standards)	(7)	Company Law, tax regulations; conceptual framework and technical bulletins contain principles and standards
China	(3)	(3)	Department of Accounting of Ministry	(7)	Economic Plan; uniform accounting system; regulations formulated by central government
Côte d'Ivoire	(3)	(3)	Comité National de la Statistique et de la Normalisation Comptable (CNSNC)	Comité National de la Statistique et de la Normalisation Comptable (CNSNC)	General Accounting Plan; Commercial Law; Foreign Capital Investment Law; Income Tax Code; Banking Law

Table IV.1 (cont.)

Country	Number of national accounting standards	Number of national auditing standards	Standard-setting body governing accounting and auditing	Compliance monitoring body	Other government laws and regulations
Cyprus	0 (1)	0 (1)			Government regulations; tax regulations; international accounting and auditing standards
Czech Republic	0.0	16	Chamber of Auditors	Supervisory Committee of Chamber of Auditors	Chart of accounts and procedures; laws on accounting and auditing
Estonia	6	8	Estonian Accounting Board, Estonian Auditing Board	Estonian Accounting Board, Estonian Auditing Board	Accounting Law 1994
Gabon	0.0	0.0	Conseil Supérieur de la Comptabilité in collaboration with Secretary General of Customs and Economic Union of Central Africa (UDEAC)	No monitoring body	General Accounting Plan 1973; Banking and Financial Institutions Accounting Plan 1979; Agricultural Accounting Plan 1981; Post Office and Telecommunications Accounting Plan 1984
Guinea	(7)	(7)	Conseil National des Normes Comptables (CNNC) and Ordre des Experts Comptables et Comptables Agréés	(7)	National Accounting Plans 1961 & 1988
India	(3)	(3)	Accounting Standards Committee of Institute of Chartered Accountants of India	(7)	Government Laws; Stock Exchange regulations; Companies Act 1956
Israel	63 in total		Institute of Certified Public Accountants develops standards, some of which are then incorporated into law	No monitoring by law as such, but Auditors' Council investigates complaints of non-compliance	Auditors' Law 1955
Lesotho	8 + IASs	4 + ISAs	Lesotho Institute of Accountants	No monitoring body as such - reliance on government	Companies Act 1967 + Amendments; Audit Act 1973
Madagascar	2	0 (4)	Ordre des Experts Comptables et Financiers et des Comptables Agréés de Madagascar; Ministry of Finance (4)	(4)	General Accounting Plan 1987; Banking Accounting Plan 1994
Malawi	3 + IASs	ISAs	Standards Committee of Council of Society of Accountants in Malawi	Standards Committee of Council of Society of Accountants in Malawi	Finance and Audit Act; international standards adopted

Table IV.1 (cont.)

Country	Number of national accounting standards	Number of national auditing standards	Standard-setting body governing accounting and auditing	Compliance monitoring body	Other government laws and regulations
Mali	0.0	0.0	Conseil National de la Comptabilité	Conseil National de la Comptabilité	Accounting Plan 1982 (based on French accounting practices); Commercial Law; General Tax Law; international standards sometimes used
Mauritania	0.0	0.0	Conseil National de la Comptabilité (6)	Compliance with standards not enforced other than by tax authorities	Mauritanian Accounting Plan 1982; Regulation 90 009 of 1990; Banking Law 1867; Taxation Law
Mauritius	20	0 (2 Guide-lines + 4 Exposure Drafts)	Mauritius Accounting and Auditing Standards Committee formulates standards and guidelines, which are published by the Minister of Finance in the Government Gazette	No monitoring body	Companies Act 1984; Stock Exchange Act 1988
Morocco	0.0	0.0	Conseil National de la Comptabilité	Ordre des Experts Comptables	Code General de la Normalisation Comptable (Moroccan Accounting Plan); Commercial Code; Taxation Law
Mozambique	(7)	(7)			Général Chart of Accounts; Commercial Law; Income Tax Code
Namibia	(3)	(3)	Public Accountants and Auditors Board of South Africa	Institute of Chartered Accountants of Namibia, in consultation with Institute of Chartered Accountants of South Africa	Companies Act, Banking Law, Stock Exchange regulations
Pakistan	IASs	ISAs	Institute of Chartered Accountants of Pakistan	(7)	Companies Ordinance 1984; Stock Exchange regulations; international accounting standards mandatory for all listed companies
Peru	2	(5)	Association of Public Accountants	Securities Commission of Peru (CONASEV)	Regulations issued by CONASEV
Russian Federation	4	1 + 9 draft	Institute at Ministry of Finance in charge of developing laws; Methodological Accounting Council of Ministry of Finance and Commission on Audit Activities under the President of the Russian Federation	Department of Methodological Accounting Council of Ministry of Finance; Commission on Audit Activities under the President of the Russian Federation; Central Bank; Rosstratnadzor	Accounting and Auditing Decrees of Russian Federation

Table IV.1 (cont.)

Country	Number of national accounting standards	Number of national auditing standards	Standard-setting body governing accounting and auditing	Compliance monitoring body	Other government laws and regulations
Senegal	(3)	25	Conseil National de la Comptabilité	Conseil National de la Comptabilité	Accounting standards based on Plan OCAM; Commercial Law; Business Corporation Law; Foreign Capital Investment Law; General Accounting Plan; Income Tax Law; Banking law
Sierra Leone	0 (1)	0 (1)	Institute of Chartered Accountants of Sierra Leone	Institute of Chartered Accountants of Sierra Leone	UK accounting laws and regulations; Companies Act, Chapter 249, of 1960
Togo	0.0	0.0	Conseil National de la Comptabilité (6)	Conseil National de la Comptabilité (6)	French accounting standards and standards based on Accounting Plan OCAM; Civil and Commercial Laws; Companies Act 1967; Foreign Capital Investment Law 1985; General Tax Law
Tunisia	0 (2)	5 + ISAs	Ordre des Experts Comptables de Tunisie in accordance with Finance Ministry	Conseil Supérieur de la Comptabilité	National Accounting Plan of 1958
Uganda	0 (1)	0 (1)	Institute of Certified Public Accountants of Uganda	No enforcement/monitoring body exists	Companies Act (Cap. 85) passed in 1958, based on UK Companies Act 1948; most qualified accountants follow standards of their international firm or professional body
Ukraine	0.0	3 + 6 draft	Ministry of Finance		Chart of Accounts; Audit Law
United Republic of Tanzania	9	10	National Board of Accountants and Auditors	National Board of Accountants and Auditors	Auditors and Accountants (Registration) Act No. 33 of 1972; Companies Ordinance, Cap. 212;; Income Tax Act 1973; TAC Act
Uzbekistan	0.0	0.0	Audit Chamber		Chart of Accounts and Regulation on Accounting (1994) are generally applied as accounting standards; Production Costs Regulation (1995)
Zambia	15	0.0	Zambia Institute of Certified Accountants	Zambia Institute of Certified Accountants	Companies Act 1994 (some minimum disclosure requirements)

IASs = International Accounting Standards.
ISAs = International Standards of Auditing.

(1) National standards to be developed.
(2) New Tunisian accounting system, developed by Conseil Supérieur de la Comptabilité, expected to be introduced in 1998.
(3) National standards exist, but number unknown.
(4) Conseil Supérieur de la Comptabilité exists but requires financing to become operational and develop national standards.
(5) National auditing standards exist, but in order to be fully adopted should be fully recognized as such by Association of Public Accountants.
(6) Body largely non-operational.
(7) Information unavailable.

Table IV.2. Use of international accounting and auditing standards

Country	International accounting standards used	International auditing standards used	How international standards are used
Bangladesh	Yes	Yes	International standards adopted by Institute of Chartered Accountants of Bangladesh and modified to meet socio-economic needs of country; national standards consistent with international standards in most areas but generally less detailed
Benin	(1)	(1)	
Botswana	Yes	Yes	International accounting and auditing standards adopted by Botswana Institute of Accountants without modification and expected to be observed (standard audit report refers to international standards)
Burkina Faso	Yes	Yes	International standards used by accountancy/audit firms when required by company investors such as World Bank
Cameroon	(1)	(1)	
Central African Republic	(1)	(1)	
Chile	Yes	(1)	National accounting standards consistent with international standards in most respects; international standards consulted when setting national standards and effort is made to avoid differences
China	Yes	Yes	International standards generally applied, but there are several principles specific to China; used in consolidated financial statements of companies listed overseas
Côte d'Ivoire	Yes	Yes	National standards based on international standards
Cyprus	Yes	Yes	Institute of Certified Public Accountants of Cyprus adopts international standards in their entirety; they are not legally required but generally followed; where no standards exist, ICPAC issues guidelines/explanatory circulars
Czech Republic	Yes	Yes	Chart of accounts and procedures are based partly on international accounting standards. International auditing standards are translated into Czech and adapted to be issued as national auditing standards
Estonia	Yes	Yes	International standards are used as the basis for accounting law and national auditing standards
Gabon	Yes	Yes	International standards used by multinational companies
Guinea	(1)	(1)	
India	Yes	Yes	National standards are consistent with international standards in most respects but are generally less detailed; effort is made to avoid differences from international standards; international standards also used in professional training

Table IV.2 (cont.)

Country	International accounting standards used	International auditing standards used	How international standards are used
Israel	Yes	Yes	International accounting standards form part of national standards and are implemented on the basis of Israeli recommendations; national auditing standards are in the process of being coordinated with IFAC standards
Lesotho	Yes	Yes	National standards are based on and consistent with international standards of IASC and IFAC
Madagascar	Yes	Yes	International standards are used, particularly by international accounting/auditing firms
Malawi	Yes	Yes	International accounting and auditing standards are adopted where appropriate and adapted as necessary to suit local accounting environment (modifications not material)
Mali	Yes	Yes	Interntaional standards are used when auditing multinational companies, etc.
Mauritania	Yes	Yes	International standards are used by subsidiaries of multinational companies and international accounting/ auditing firms, and when required by investors
Mauritius	Yes	Yes	National accounting and auditing standards and guidelines are formulated using UK ASC, IASC and IFAC pronouncements as a guide
Morocco	Yes	Yes	International accounting standards respected by Moroccan Accounting Plan; also used in consolidated annual reports of listed companies, where national rules are silent/ flexible, in accordance with requirements of international investors and in professional education
Mozambique	(1)	(1)	
Namibia	Yes	Yes	Institute of Chartered Accountants of Namibia adopts pronouncements issued by the Institute of Chartered Accountants of South Africa, which are based on international standards and GAAP
Pakistan	Yes	Yes	Use of international accounting standards is mandatory for all listed companies
Peru	Yes	Yes	National standards are consistent with international standards; international accounting standards are used widely in consolidated accounts of listed companies and where national accounting standards are flexible or non-existent
Russian Federation	Yes	Yes	National standards are generally developed on the basis of international standards and EU Directives
Senegal	Yes	Yes	International standards are referred to when formulating national standards and used by international accounting firms and subsidiaries of multinational companies

Table IV.2 (cont.)

Country	International accounting standards used	International auditing standards used	How international standards are used
Sierra Leone	Yes	Yes	International accounting standards and standards of the Accountancy Bodies of West Africa (ABWA) are adopted and modified as considered necessary; national standards are being developed and reference is made to international standards International standards are used by practising firms and also by other large companies, especially banks and insurance companies
Togo	Yes	Yes	Voluntary use of international standards
Tunisia	No	Yes	There is currently no obligation to follow international accounting standards; however, a new Tunisian accounting system should be introduced in 1998 and should comply with international accounting standards International auditing standards are used by members of Ordre des Experts Comptables de Tunisie
Uganda	Yes	No	Multinational companies adopt those international standards advised by their parent
Ukraine	Yes	Yes	International standards are referred to when setting national standards; attempts are made to avoid differences from international standards
United Republic of Tanzania	Yes	Yes	International standards are used as a basis for formulating national standards and are adopted where no national accounting/auditing standard exists; national standards are generally less detailed
Uzbekistan	Yes	No	International accounting standards are used as a basis for the Production Cost Regulation and the Draft of the new Accounting Law; also used by foreign companies and joint ventures
Zambia	Yes	No	International accounting standards are adopted as national standards where appropriate, sometimes with modification; consideration soon to be given to adopting international auditing standards.

(1) Information unavailable.

Table IV.3. Professional ethics

Country	Code of professional ethics	Body responsible for implementation of code of professional ethics
Bangladesh	Yes	Disciplinary Committee of Institute of Chartered Accountants of Bangladesh, Council of Institute of Cost and Management Accountants of Bangladesh
Benin	(1)	
Botswana	Yes	Botswana Institute of Accountants
Burkina Faso	No	
Cameroon	(1)	
Central African Republic	(1)	
Chile	Yes	(1)
China	Yes	Department of Accounting of Ministry of Finance (accounting); China Institute of Certified Public Accountants (auditing)
Côte d'Ivoire	Yes	Ordre des Experts Comptables et Comptables Agréés
Cyprus	No (2)	
Czech Republic	Yes	Chamber of Auditors of the Czech Republic
Estonia	Yes	Estonian Auditing Board
Gabon	No	
Guinea	(1)	
India	(1)	
Israel	Yes	Institute of Certified Public Accountants, Auditors' Council
Lesotho	Yes	Lesotho Institute of Accountants
Madagascar	Yes	Ordre des Experts Comptables et Financiers et des Comptables Agréés de Madagascar
Malawi	Yes	Society of Accountants in Malawi
Mali	Yes	Ordre des Comptables Agréés et Experts Comptables du Mali
Mauritania	Yes	Ordre National des Experts Comptables Mauritaniens; Disciplinary Committee of Ministry of Finance
Mauritius	Yes	UK accountancy bodies (ACCA, ICAEW, CIMA)
Morocco	Yes	Ordre des Experts Comptables
Mozambique	(1)	
Namibia	Yes	Public Accountants and Auditors Board (Namibia)
Pakistan	Yes	Institute of Chartered Accountants of Pakistan
Peru	Yes	Ethics Committee of Association of Public Accountants

Table IV.3 (cont.)

Country	Code of professional ethics	Body responsible for implementation of code of professional ethics
Russian Federation	(1)	
Senegal	Yes	Board of Ordre National des Experts et Evaluateurs Agréés du Sénégal; President of Court of Appeal
Sierra Leone	Yes	Institute of Chartered Accountants of Sierra Leone
Togo	No (4)	
Tunisia	Yes	Ordre des Experts Comptables de Tunisie
Uganda	No (5)	
Ukraine	(1)	
United Republic of Tanzania	Yes (3)	National Board of Accountants and Auditors, Tanzania Association of Accountants
Uzbekistan	No	
Zambia	Yes	Zambia Institute of Certified Accountants

(1) Information unavailable.
(2) Proposed legislation (expected to be passed in 1996) provides for a code to be implemented by the new Council.
(3) Currently two codes exist; however, the intention is to develop one single code based on the IFAC code of conduct.
(4) Ethical code of Ordre des Experts Comptables (France) is generally respected.
(5) Code in the process of being drafted by the Institute of Certified Public Accountants of Uganda.

CHAPTER VII

CURRENT DEVELOPMENTS IN ENVIRONMENTAL ACCOUNTING[1]

SUMMARY

Environmental accounting rules are being actively developed on a worldwide basis. This chapter reviews developments in four areas: financial accounting; managerial accounting; accounting for physical flows; and environmental reporting. In so far as environmental issues have a financially quantifiable effect and can be captured within established generally accepted accounting principles (GAAP), a measure of consensus on rules in the area of financial accounting is gradually being achieved. This chapter identifies those aspects of international GAAP where there is general agreement and those where more work is required. In the field of managerial accounting, current efforts are directed mainly at the issue of full-cost accounting. They typically fall into two categories: recommendations for more detailed conventional cost accounting, and recommendations for the internalization of external costs. More progress is being made on the former than the latter. This chapter also identifies initiatives in accounting for physical flows. In the area of environmental reporting there is a great variety in terms of the format and content of reports, and the conclusion is drawn that greater encouragement needs to be given to achieving comparability.

I. INTRODUCTION AND BACKGROUND

A. Introduction

An ad hoc meeting of the Intergovernmental Working Group of Experts on International Standards of Accounting and Reporting (ISAR) was held from 6 to 8 December 1995 as a follow-up to the thirteenth annual session of the Group. Environmental accounting was the sole topic of the meeting. The following experts were present:

Mr. Roger Adams
Chartered Association of
Certified Accountants
United Kingdom

Mr. Matteo Bartolomeo
Fondazione Eni Enrico Mattei
Italy

Ms. Jan Bebbington
   University of Dundee
   United Kingdom

Ms. Nancy Bennet
   United Nations Environment Programme

Mr. Mozammal Hoque
   Institute of Chartered Accountants of
   Bangladesh

Mr. Ferid El Kobbi
   Ministry of Finance
   Tunisia

Mr. David Moore
   Canadian Institute of Chartered Accountants
   Canada

Mr. Johan Piet
   Fédération des Experts Comptables Européens
   Belgium

One of the major purposes of the meeting was to determine specifically what further contribution UNCTAD could make to the field of environmental accounting. At the thirteenth session of ISAR it had been decided that in the interest of harmonization, ISAR should assess the many developments and produce a conceptual framework/guidance for national standard-setters and other interested parties. This could help them to avoid duplicating their efforts in devising different solutions for the same problems.

The ad hoc meeting spent three days discussing four areas within the field of what is loosely called "environmental accounting": financial accounting; management accounting, including full-cost accounting; environmental reporting, including environmental performance indicators; and environmental auditing. It also discussed a project proposal to raise funds for the activities which would allow ISAR to develop the guidelines.

The following sections provide an overview of current developments in the field of environmental accounting. The survey upon which this chapter was based identified current environmental accounting guidance and research that have been completed or are currently being undertaken around the world, and analysed those areas which have been investigated comprehensively and those which have not. The meeting considered the feasibility of developing a possible "conceptual framework" for environmental accounting. This subject matter and format of the report could be used as the basis for this conceptual framework as the chapter identifies and analyses current worldwide initiatives in the field of environmental accounting. There is an underlying assumption throughout the chapter that "sustainable development" is the ultimate goal of both governments and corporations.

B. Framework, general issues and structure of the chapter

A review of the literature involving the phrase *"environmental accounting"* shows that it appears to mean different things to different people. At the *national income accounting level* it has variously been interpreted as referring to physical inventories of natural resources, to the financial costs of environmental degradation and related defensive expenditures, and to the computation of a true (or green) GDP. At the *corporate level* the phrase may be used in the context of internal (management) accounting techniques, financial accounting for external reporting purposes, and the input/output analysis of physical throughputs.

Rather than adopt a discrete, country-by-country approach, this chapter takes as a starting point one particular framework within which current developments can be placed. The United States Environmental Protection Agency (EPA) has produced the following representation of the environmental accounting universe:

Table VII.1.   A framework for environmental accounting

Type of environmental accounting	Focus	Audience
(1) National income accounting	Nation	External
(2) Financial accounting	Firm	External
(3) Managerial or management accounting	Firm, division, facility, product line or system	Internal

Source: Environmental Protection Agency, An introduction to *Environmental Accounting as a Business Management* Tool (Washington, D.C., 1995).

It should be noted, however, that this framework excludes consideration of the nature of the measurement unit(s) employed. A refinement of the EPA framework might be:

Table VII.2.   The EPA environmental accounting framework modified

Type of environmental accounting	Focus	Audience	Measurement unit
(1) National income accounting	Nation	External	(i) Physical (ii) Financial
(2) Financial accounting	Firm	External	(i) Financial
(3) Managerial or management accounting	Firm, division, facility, product line or system	Internal	(i) Physical (ii) Financial

Any attempts to develop the EPA framework outlined above, or to develop a separate conceptual framework for environmental accounting would, certainly have to incorporate qualitative elements for financial accounting, such as relevance, objectivity, timeliness, accuracy and verifiability, as contained in the conceptual framework for financial accounting developed by ISAR, the International Accounting Standards Committee (IASC), the Financial Accounting Standards Board (FASB) and others.

It is only a small step from environmental accounting to environmental reporting. Without an obligation to report (internally or externally) on environmental activities, it is doubtful whether environmental accounting techniques would have reached even the elementary stage they appear to have reached. Environmental reporting is not the primary focus of this survey, but it is necessary to remember that extensions in reporting requirements tend to drive the underlying accounting methods. Several frameworks for environmental reporting have been published. These and other environmental reporting issues are dealt with in section IV below.

Although national income accounting is identified as part of the EPA framework in table VII.1 above, this chapter does not deal with environmental accounting at the public sector level, the System of National Accounts (SNA - United Nations, 1968), or with the subsequent updating of the SNA via a System for Integrated Environmental and Economic Accounting (SEEA - as developed in 1993 by the Statistical Division of the Department of Economic and Social Affairs, United Nations). A recent report by the World Wildlife Foundation *Real Value for Nature* (1995) provides a comprehensive critique of the current method of computation of Gross Domestic Product (GDP). However, this topic is beyond the mandate of ISAR, although interest has been expressed in the relationship between environmental accounting at the national level and environmental accounting at the corporate level.

The relationship between environmental accounting and environmental auditing is very close, but there is not space here to describe developments in environmental auditing and environmental verification. Suffice to say that when considering the qualitative characteristics of environmental accounting data it will be necessary to invoke a "verifiability" criterion at all times.

II. FINANCIAL ACCOUNTING

A. Environmental issues as a part of traditional financial accounting

Traditional financial accounting and reporting are influenced and constrained in equal measure by a number of factors, which are outlined below.

1. Developed GAAP frameworks and the need for an environmental accounting framework

There seems to be a consensus in GAAP worldwide as to the recognition and measurement issues relating to environmental (actual and contingent) liabilities, provisions and expected recoveries. This is examined in more detail below. Currently, work is under way to develop an environmental reporting framework, for example the work being carried out by the environmental task force of the Fédération des Experts Comptables Européens (FEE).

2. Domestic legislative requirements (financial or environmental)

At the same time as international GAAP are converging on environmental liability and provisioning issues, domestic disclosure requirements appear to be acting *so as to limit* the application of environmental accounting techniques for other financial accounting purposes. In particular, the widespread absence of *explicit environmental disclosure requirements* combines with the conventional application of the *materiality concept* to ensure that - apart from liabilities, provisions, contingent liabilities and expected recoveries - little quantitative environmental accounting data appear in corporate annual reports as a matter of course.

Fortunately, and largely because of the influence of the United States Securities and Exchange Commission (SEC) and EPA regulators, an increasing amount of data on environmental operating costs and capital expenditures is being disclosed in the financial review (management discussion and analysis (MD & A)) section of the annual reports of companies with American listings. Generally, however, companies appear unwilling to make meaningful environmental risk assessments a standard part of their financial review.

3. Corporate willingness to undertake discretionary disclosures

Corporate willingness to undertake discretionary disclosure activity (financial or environmental) appears to be strongly influenced by the possibility (or probability in some cases) of litigation arising as a result of discretionary (or non-prudential) disclosures. Evidence of corporate reluctance to disclose potential environmental liabilities is partially anecdotal, but many published case studies refer to the need for corporations to involve their legal advisers (in addition to their auditors) in any decisions regarding estimation (and disclosure) of environmental liabilities. Most financial environmental accounting begins in earnest only when the following two conditions occur simultaneously:

> (a)   the probability of a liability (as defined in the conventional GAAP framework) has reached the level where a provision or a contingent liability note is necessary if the accounts are to escape without a qualified audit report; and
>
> (b)   the conventional financial materiality threshold has been crossed by the potential liability.

When only one of these conditions is met, recognition and subsequent disclosure may not occur.

Table VII.3.   Governmental or professional bodies issuing guidance on the treatment of environmental costs within established GAAP

Initiating body	Document
United States - Securities and Exchange Commission (SEC)	FRR 36, "Interpretative Release on Management's Discussion and Analysis" (guidance on disclosure of environmental liabilities) Staff Accounting Bulletin (SAB) 92, "Interpretation of GAAP regarding Contingent Liabilities"
United States - Financial Accounting Standards Board (FASB)	FAS 5, "Accounting for Contingencies" FIN 14, "Reasonable Estimation of the Amount of a Loss" EITF 89 - 13, "Accounting for the Costs of Asbestos Removal" EITF 90 - 8, "Capitalization of Costs to Treat Environmental Contamination" EITF 93 - 5, "Accounting for Environmental Liabilities" GASB 18, "Accounting for Municipal Solid Waste Landfill Closure and Post-Closure Care Costs"
United States - Environmental Protection Agency (EPA)	An Introduction to Environmental Accounting as a Business Management Tool"
United States - American Institute of Certified Public Accountants (AICPA)	(Draft) Statement of Position on "Environmental Remediation Liabilities"
Canada - Canadian Institute of Chartered Accountants (CICA)	Section 3060 CICA Handbook, Future Removal and Site Restoration Costs Environmental Costs and Liabilities: Accounting and Financial Reporting Issues Project in motion: "Environmental Costs"
Australia: Australian Accounting Research Foundation (AARF) and Australian Accounting Standards Review Board (ASRB)	ASRB 102, "Accounting for the Extractive Industries" Urgent Issues Group (Abstract 4) - "Disclosure of Accounting Policies for Restoration Obligations in the Extractive Industries"
United Kingdom - Institute of Chartered Accountants in England and Wales (ICAEW)	"Financial Reporting of Environmental Liabilities: A Discussion Paper"
Europe - European Commission's Accounting Advisory Forum (ECAFF)	"Environmental Issues in Financial Reporting" (Draft only)

B. Current initiatives in financial environmental accounting

Until quite recently, accounting standard-setters generally seem to have taken the view that existing accounting standards deal satisfactorily with the majority of environment-related issues, such as recognition, measurement and disclosure, particularly of contingent liabilities and provisions. Thus standards such as the United States FAS 5, Accounting for Contingencies, have not been revised to contain explicit reference to the environment.

Current initiatives in the field of financial accounting for environmental costs and liabilities have, however, begun to recognize that increased levels of disclosure may be appropriate and that additional guidance may be necessary in order to amplify or interpret existing standards.

Table VII.4.   Environmental accounting issues and proposed GAAP-based solutions

Environmental accounting issue	Common proposed solutions
Definition of environmental costs and expenses	Costs of environmental measures + environmental losses (CICA and ICAEW) Environmental costs which losses do not lead to future expected benefits (losses, fines etc.)
Environmental cost recognition and measurement issues	Materiality, measurability, certainty (IASC framework)
Capital or revenue allocation problem	Capitalize if it is intended to prevent or reduce future environmental damage or to conserve resources (ECAAF and ICAEW) Judgemental allocation may be necessary (ICAEW and EPA)
Capitalization of environmental costs incurred subsequent to the acquisition of a capital asset	Capitalize either: (i) if costs result in an increase in expected future economic benefits; or (ii) if costs are considered to be a cost of expected future benefits from the asset, irrespective of whether there are any increased economic benefits (CICA and ICAEW)
Accounting for future environmental costs	Where an entity has a legal obligation, or is otherwise committed, to incur future expenditure, the costs involved represent an environmental liability (ICAEW)
Estimation (and continuous revision) of environmental liabilities and provisions	Disclosure precedes accounting recognition Normal contingency estimation procedures: probability, best estimate Annual revisions where appropriate charged to current year (FASB and ICAEW)
Accounting for expected recoveries	No set-off permitted: recoveries should be accounted for separately (SEC, FASB and ICAEW)
Accounting for the impairment of assets	Reduce the carrying amount of the asset rather than introduce a liability (ICAEW) CICA approach might involve a loss accrual
The disclosure of environmental risk environmental risks	Use of MD & A in the United States or operating and financial review disclosure (OFR), which is the United Kingdom's requirement, to discuss significant issues facing an entity (SEC and Accounting Standards Board (ASB) in the United Kingdom)
Environmental accounting policy disclosures	All significant accounting policies relating to financial statement items to be disclosed May not give rise to a policy disclosure regarding environmental issues
Operation of the materiality concept	Normal application - not amended in any way because of environmental issues (however, is this a correct approach?)
Other disclosures	The unique nature of environmental costs and liabilities is not a sufficient criterion for separate disclosure (ICAEW) ECAFF and FEE suggest disclosure of environmental losses (is this a GAAP issue?)

The major environment-related financial accounting issues identified in the above-mentioned studies, and the solutions currently being offered, are set out in VII.4, along with some of the solutions suggested. There is already a great deal of commonality between the solutions offered to financial accounting problems raised by environmental issues.

Given the amount of groundwork which has already been done, it should not be difficult for an international accountancy body such as ISAR or IASC to pull all the various threads together to provide authoritative guidance in this important area.

C. A framework for the recognition and measurement of potential environmental liabilities

Recognition and measurement of a potential environmental liability is probably the central point of the financial environmental accounting debate. Preliminary guidance on this topic is given in the United Nations publication *International Accounting and Reporting Issues: 1991 Review*.[2] Attempts are being made to develop a framework within which the recognition question can be handled. The American Institute of Certified Public Accountants (AICPA) is developing a statement of position on environmental remediation liabilities which recommends that the estimation of a liability should be evaluated as each of the following benchmarks occurs:

(a)   identification and verification of an entity as a potentially responsible party;
(b)   receipt of a unilateral administrative order; participation, as a potentially responsible party, in the remedial investigation and feasibility study;
(d)   completion of the feasibility study;
(e)   issuance of a Record of Decision, which is a statement by the EPA to the effect that it agrees with the procedures which a corporation used to assess the extent of the environmental clean-up action which needs to be undertaken; and
(f)   remedial design through operation and maintenance, including post-remediation monitoring.

At each stage, argues the AICPA, changes in liability estimates should be accounted for under APB Opinion 20, Changes in Accounting Estimates. A similar "staged" approach to liability management was demonstrated in a recent article in *Management Accounting* (August 1995), based on the approach used by Chevron[3] in the United States. In general terms, and with the inclusion of opinions of various countries, a framework for recognition and measurement might include some of the following steps:

Table VII.5. Stages in the environmental liability recognition and measurement process

Stages in the recognition and measurement process	Issues to be considered
1. The entity becomes aware that an environmental remediation liability may exist	Recognition depends on the existence of a (legal) obligation: how is this defined?
2. Attempts should be made to estimate the potential liability	Use of multidisciplinary teams including finance and environmental experts: are precise estimates ever possible?
3. In the absence of any hard information a contingent liability note or other disclosure should be issued	Should this disclosure be in the financial review section or in the notes to the financial statements, or both?
4. As information becomes available estimates should be recognized in the accounts	What cost items go towards making up these estimates?
5. Changes in estimates should be recognized annually	How should changes in estimates be disclosed?
6. An overall summary of environmental liability position should be given in the financial review section	How frank should such disclosures be?

Several standard-setting bodies - the ASB in the United Kingdom and ASRB in Australia - have initiated projects dealing with provisioning. The Australian project will deal with provisions for environmental costs, including restoration and decommissioning. The FASB has a separate project dealing with nuclear decommissioning.

III. MANAGERIAL ENVIRONMENTAL ACCOUNTING ISSUES

A. Introduction

Developments in internal (managerial) environmental accounting are not subject to the same degree of institutional guidance and enforcement as are the financial accounting developments described above. Most of the published work on internal environmental accounting appears to be focused on the corporate sector.

The most active *institutional* bodies dealing with internal environmental costs appear to be the EPA and the CICA. Much of the activity in this area is now being carried out by individual companies. The main source for information on developments in this area is the publication *Green Ledgers: Case Studies in Corporate Environmental Accounting*, published by the World Resources Institute in 1995. Companies featured in this review include Amoco, Ciba-Geigy, Dow Chemical, Du Pont and S C Johnson Wax. The final report of the CICA's major project on full-cost accounting was due to be delivered in 1996. Also in Canada, utility companies such as Ontario Hydro and BC Hydro are reportedly well advanced with full-cost accounting experiments.

Much of the work currently going on in the internal (managerial) environmental accounting field can be summarized under two headings: improving private environmental cost allocations and internalizing external (societal) costs.

B. Improved environmental cost allocation

As an alternative to the use of the "stakeholder and decision usefulness" approach implicit in financial reporting, internal accounting demands the adoption of a "cost-based" perspective.

The EPA has provided a useful framework for environmental cost analysis. It tries to identify the various ways in which environmental costs might arise (see table VII.6).

Table VII.6.   A framework for environmental cost classification

EPA environmental cost classification	Examples of environmental costs included
Private costs	**Conventional costs** (equipment, labour, materials) **Potentially hidden costs** (regulatory: systems, monitoring, levies) (upfront: site studies, installations) (back-end: decommissioning, site surveys) (voluntary: audits, reports, R&D, landscaping) **Contingent costs** (penalties, fines, remediation) **Image & relationship costs** (corporate image and relationships)
Societal costs [externalities]	Cost incurred by society at large which are not "charged back" to the responsible entity and which therefore do not impact on the "bottom line" of that entity

It then suggests which environmental costs can be better identified and allocated more accurately within the conventional cost accounting system. As already noted above, this approach does not involve the internalization of external (societal) costs.

C. Internalizing external (societal) costs and full-cost accounting

Recent research and commentaries relating to societal or full-cost accounting have been undertaken by:

(a)   the United Nations publication *Accounting for Sustainable Forestry Management: A Case Study* (UNCTAD/DTCI/4);

(b)   the report *Incentives and Disincentives for the Adoption of Sustainable Development by Transnational Corporations* (TD/B/ITNC/AC.1/3);

(c)   the CICA full-cost accounting project, mentioned previously;

(d)   the EPA environmental accounting project;

(e)   developments in "design for the environment" (DFE - such as pioneered by AT&T);

(f)   individual full-cost accounting corporate initiatives (e.g. Ontario Hydro);

(g)   the Government of the United Kingdom's Advisory Committee on Business and the Environment (ACBE) working group on full-cost accounting;

(h)   the "net value added" approach to financial reporting of the Dutch corporation BSO Origin; and

(i)   the Business Council for Sustainable Development's paper "Internalizing Environmental Costs to Promote Eco-Efficiency" (1994).

Although there appears to be a great deal of activity in this area, progress on full-cost accounting is in general not as rapid as comparable progress in the financial accounting and financial reporting field. The EPA says that:

> "Efforts to integrate societal costs into business decisions will continue and expand. Most corporate information and decision systems do not currently support such proactive and prospective decision making... Although some companies are at the leading edge to address societal costs, it will likely be some time before societal impacts and costs can be integrated into cost allocation, capital budgeting, process and product design, and general business decisions. However, there is a growing body of information documenting a variety of businesses engaged in advancing the state of the art to bring societal costs into their decision making."[4]

The BSO Origin experiment with the clean-up costs of its emissions - deducting these societal costs from conventional value added - has been widely applauded but has not been copied. There appears to be considerable doubt as to the reliability of the cost data. Since these "green accounts" are in "memorandum" form only, it is not possible to see how they impact - if at all - on product pricing and corporate strategy.

The Advisory Committee on Business and the Environment (ACBE) has formed a study group to consider the issue of internalizing external costs. At the time of writing the group has not reported, but there are strong indications that their position will be similar to that expressed by the EPA. Thus, given the various problems involved - competitiveness, measurement, valuation etc. - individual corporate experiments at the voluntary level are likely to precede any major institutional initiatives.

The CICA has sponsored a major project on full-cost accounting; it was expected to report in early 1996.

Discussion at ISAR's thirteenth session confirmed that issues such as international competitiveness and management's willingness to change are major stumbling blocks to widespread adoption of full-cost accounting techniques on a voluntary basis.

D. Mass balance and physical inventory accounting

The notion of "continuous environmental improvement" implies a detailed knowledge of product life cycles and production processes. Accounting systems are being developed to deal with the need to control and account for physical flows of materials, products and wastes.

This year's ISAR session received information on the integrated environmental accounting methodology being developed by the Italian organization Fondazione Eni Enrico Mattei (FEEM). An alternative physical accounting methodology, called "mass and energy flow costs accounting", is being developed by the Ecological Economics Research Institute (IOW, Germany) and, like the Italian project, is being field-tested in a number of active companies.

Many European companies use the mass balance (*oko-bilanz*) methodology as the central feature of their environmental reporting process (see, for example, Det Danske Stalvalsevearke, Kunert AG and Landesgirokasse). The practice does not appear to be common in North American or British environmental reporting. It would be interesting to compare the work being done on full-cost accounting in the United States by the EPA and others with the physical environmental accounting methodologies already in use in Europe.

IV. ENVIRONMENTAL REPORTING

A. Environmental reporting: A definition

For the purposes of this chapter environmental reporting can be understood to be the publication or provision of environmental information concerning an entity's environmental policies, commitments and performance. Publication or provision is (largely) voluntary and the information can be distinguished from the financially quantified information discussed in section II of this report, which is generally demanded by GAAP or by statute. Only in Denmark is the disclosure of environmental data through the annual reporting corporate package required by law.

Environmental reporting does not necessarily assume that the shareholders and investors are the principal stakeholder group. Consequently, it may be found in the annual corporate report, a stand-alone environmental performance report, or single site reports or employee newsletters.

B. The spread of environmental reporting

Environmental liability, risk and performance data are now communicated by a significant number of international companies. Estimates vary, but probably somewhere in excess of 500 companies worldwide have now produced stand-alone environmental performance reports, although these are not always produced annually. Environmental reporting appears to be particularly strong in North America and Northern and Western Europe. Most companies wishing to make non-financial environmental disclosures have chosen to do so in an independent corporate environmental performance report. The number of such reports does not appear to be diminishing. Further details of the nature and extent of environmental reporting can be found in the United Nations reports *Environmental Disclosures: International Survey of Corporate Reporting Practices* (E/C.10/AC.3/1992/3 and E/C.10/AC.3/1994/4).

A much greater number of listed companies[5] (over 50 per cent in the United Kingdom) make some limited form of environmental disclosure via their financial statements. Few companies release more than their environmental policies and general statements as to corporate commitment.

An increasing number of companies worldwide (for example, Norsk-Hydro, BSO Origin, Det Danske Stalvalsevearke, Thorn EMI) are disclosing non-financial environmental data *within* the annual reporting package but outside the audited part of the annual report. These disclosures are usually reasonably detailed summaries of their environmental performance, although there is no consistency from company to company.

C. Environmental reporting models

There are two major disclosure approaches in use (categorized by Elkington as the "Rhine Model"and the "Atlantic Model" (United Nations Environment Programme, *Company Environmental Reporting: A measure of the Progress of Business and Industry towards Sustainable Development*, SustainAbility, 1994):

Table VII.7.   Environmental reporting models

The "Rhine Model"	The eco-balance (*oko-bilanz*) or mass balance approach: physical inputs and outputs are recorded and disclosed in a balance sheet format
The "Atlantic Model"	The systems and compliance with standards approach: environmental management systems are described, compliance with external legislation is attested and performance targets are set and/or reported on

Such non-financial disclosures derive from internal environmental accounting or management systems. It is possible that the apparent divergence in reporting approaches described immediately above echoes regional differences already noted in the area of financial reporting. More research is required in order to determine whether financial and non-financial environmental disclosure patterns replicate existing financial reporting practices.

D. Environmental reporting frameworks and guidelines

A number of sets of environmental reporting guidelines have been published. ISAR has indicated items which could be considered for disclosure.[6] The guidelines represent an independent review of current best practices, fall comfortably within the current financial reporting framework and are practical. The guidelines include disclosure of accounting policies and the identification of income, expenditures, investment and liabilities (actual and contingent) related to environmental matters. Other recommendations exist, probably the best known being the Public Environmental Reporting Initiative (PERI), which originated in the United States. In addition, guidance has been issued by the World Industry Council for the Environment (WICE) and by the United Kingdom's Confederation of British Industry. These reporting frameworks are analysed in *Company Environmental Reporting: a Measure of the Progress of Business and Industry towards Sustainable Development* (P28 Technical Report No.24, United Nations Environment Programme/SustainAbility, Paris, 1994, ISBN 92-8078-1413-9).

Major surveys of environmental reporting have been carried out in Canada (CICA), the United Kingdom (KPMG), Switzerland (Ellipson), and Germany (IOW), on a worldwide basis and on a European basis (by the United Nations in the previously mentioned reports and by OKAY in the United Kingdom).

E. Further developments in environmental reporting

New developments in environmental reporting include:

(a)　the sectoral benchmarking of environmental performance. In the United Kingdom, for example, the chemicals industry produces an annual report on "indicators of performance". Given the number of stand-alone environmental reports issued by companies in sectors such as oil, gas, petroleum, chemicals, water and telecommunications, there is obviously scope for greater experimentation in this area;

(b)　the construction of company-specific indices of environmental performance, for example by Novo Nordisk (Denmark), Rhône-Poulenc (France) and Det Danske Stalvalseverke (Denmark).

F. Environmental reporting and the financial sector

Financial statements are aimed primarily at the shareholder and financial investor community. There is considerable interest at present regarding the degree of importance which the financial sector attaches to environmental disclosures.

In the United States, the proactive stance of the SEC and the EPA can be interpreted as evidence of the importance which regulators attach to adequate and appropriate environmental disclosures. The apparent closeness of the relationship between these two regulatory bodies means that corporations filing for SEC purposes are probably subject to the most intense environmental scrutiny in the world. Comparisons between United States filing data and United Kingdom filing data show that jointly listed companies produce far more environmental liability detail for the SEC than they do for the London Stock Exchange.

In the United Kingdom, the London Stock Exchange has not demanded environmental disclosures as a precondition for listing purposes. Research into the real environmental concerns of investment analysts and fund managers has so far proved somewhat inconclusive (according to a joint study undertaken in 1994 by Business in the Environment (BiE) and Extel, a stock exchange information service). It may be supposed that the financial sector will become more directly interested in the output of the environmental reporting process when there is increased comparability and when formal sectoral benchmarking becomes commonplace.

However, the European Federation of Financial Analysts' Societies has published a paper - "Environmental Reporting and Disclosures: The Financial Analyst's Views" - which strongly endorses the need for an enhanced level of environmental performance communication between corporations and analysts.

G. Independent attestation of environmental reporting

Environmental reporting goes largely unattested. Where there is some form of attestation, it is generally unique, and cannot be compared. The role of the accounting profession in the environmental attestation process is ambivalent: as many, if not more, verifiers' reports appear to be issued by firms of environmental consultants as by large accounting firms. It is likely that the criteria for verifiers included in the European Union's Eco Management and Audit Scheme (EMAS) regulation will operate to exclude many accounting firms from the role of environmental verifier.

Research into the form and content of verifiers' reports is being conducted in the United Kingdom by the Institute of Chartered Accountants in England and Wales (ICAEW) and by the FEE in Europe.

H. Environmental reporting as an integral part of overall corporate governance

Given the worldwide interest in the financial aspects of corporate governance, ISAR might wish to consider ways of developing the theme of corporate environmental governance. This approach is being considered in the United Kingdom as a means of encouraging environmental reporting without actually legislating for it.

V. CONCLUSIONS

A. Financial accounting

There appears to be some measure of agreement concerning general recognition and measurement issues in respect of environmental liabilities, provisions and expected recoveries. Organizations such as the SEC, FASB and AICPA (in the United States), the ASB and the ICAEW (in the United Kingdom), the CICA (in Canada) and the European Commission's Accounting Advisory Forum have produced, or are in the process of producing, statements dealing with environmental liabilities and provisions.

There is less agreement concerning the identification, measurement and separate disclosure of environmental risks and costs (revenue or capital). This lack of consistency arises (a) because of straightforward estimation and allocation difficulties, and (b) because separate disclosure of such costs is often not formally required either by statute or by international standard-setting organizations.

Apart from estimated recoveries from other potentially responsible parties, there appears to be no concerted attempt to quantify the financial benefits flowing from environmentally beneficial corporate behaviour.

It is debatable whether there is a need for a separate environmental accounting conceptual framework dealing exclusively with financial accounting and reporting issues. Given the considerable amount of groundwork which has already been done, it would seem more appropriate for a body to issue an accounting standard or guidelines in this area, and to link it or them to previous pronouncements (e.g. accounting for contingencies/the conceptual framework project).

B. Managerial environmental accounting

Improved internal cost allocation of private environmental costs can lead to greater awareness of entities' environmental impact, and as a consequence may prompt a behavioural change.

Internalizing external (societal) environmental costs poses difficulties for entities because of measurement and valuation problems on the one hand, and national and international competitiveness on the other. Experimentation at the corporate level is likely to be a productive way forward. Furthermore, improved internal cost allocation of private environmental costs may be an important adjunct or even a starting point for many firms to tackle this challenging issue. Environmental considerations should play a major part in all investment decisions.

At least one major research project for full-cost accounting is under way (in Canada) and several North American companies are undertaking testing. There may be scope for comparing the environmental accounting methodologies being developed in corporate North America with the experiments taking place in Europe.

C. Environmental reporting

Environmental liability, risk and performance data are now communicated by a significant number of international companies. There are clear regional and philosophical differences in current environmental reporting techniques.

Despite the growth of disclosure, there are no authoritative non-financial disclosure standards, and there is thus little comparability.

Environmental reporting goes largely unattested. Where there is some form of attestation, it is generally unique, and cannot be compared. The role of the accounting profession in the environmental attestation process is ambivalent.

It is still difficult to identify the "drivers" which prompt environmental information disclosure. It is likely that environmental reporting will continue to occur in different formats (such as consolidated performance reporting, site-based reporting, staff reporting and financial-statement-based reporting). Environmental reporting frameworks may be developed for each and all of these stakeholder groups.

A number of relatively similar environmental reporting frameworks have already been developed. This is another area where ISAR might consider developing core guidance.

Given the worldwide interest in the financial aspects of corporate governance, ISAR should consider ways of developing the theme of corporate environmental governance.

After analysing the foregoing report and discussion, the participants in the December ad hoc meeting concluded that in the field of financial accounting two activities were useful and necessary. First, a synthesis should be made of the recommendations of bodies such as the American Institute of Certified Public Accountants, the Financial Accounting Standards Board, the Securities and Exchange Commission in the United States; the Accounting Standards Board and the Institute of Chartered Accountants in England and Wales; the Australian Accounting Research Standards Board; the Canadian Institute of Chartered Accountants; and the advisory forum of the European Commission. Ongoing research should also be considered. Where there were differences of opinion, they should be discussed at the meetings of expert working groups. These findings could be supplemented by case studies of best practice, for example in the area of estimation of liabilities. Work on this assignment has begun and the fifteenth session of ISAR will review the report.

Second, work should be undertaken which would go beyond the conventional financial accounting model. For example, this might include making the link between financial performance and environmental performance. One could assess what environmental performance indicators were in use, which were the most meaningful and how they could be linked to financial performance. It was suggested that industry associations, financial analysts and the United Nations Environment Programme (UNEP) be involved in this effort. In addition, the group noted that significant financial environmental information (such as environmental performance indicators and information about environmental risk) might be contained in the annual report or in the management discussion and analysis report, which reached a wider audience. The aim of this work might be to develop a few indicators that could be recommended for use. The fifteenth session of ISAR will also review the report on this subject.

In the area of environmental management accounting it was suggested that a review be undertaken of the state of the art. It was felt that long-term improvements in financial accounting would come through better management accounting. Also, the bridge to accounting for sustainable development might well be through management accounting. In fact, the group felt that this was the most dynamic area of environmental accounting. While there are a variety of practices in conventional cost accounting and full-cost accounting, not much is disseminated about their actual application since the experimentation takes place at the company level and contributes to the enterprise's competitive advantage. A number of company surveys of best practices have already been undertaken. The Fondazione Eni Enrico Mattei (FEEM) is undertaking a survey and in-depth case studies to produce a framework for those enterprises wishing to improve environmental cost accounting. This survey focuses on Europe and North America, and ISAR could possibly contribute to its globalization. It was suggested that once the FEEM framework had been developed, UNCTAD and UNEP work with FEEM for its testing and dissemination, particularly in developing countries. This could be done by means of workshops and intensive training courses in managerial accounting. It was suggested that UNCTAD study the need to produce a handbook of best practices.

Furthermore, it was suggested that it would be useful to undertake a survey of existing environmental reporting guidelines. In particular, attention should be paid to the applicability of these guidelines to small and medium-sized enterprises since there is little in the field that specifically addresses their needs. Participants felt that the quality of reports in general varied widely and that further research into their usefulness was needed. A project is under way at UNEP to determine exactly what some users (such as banks and non-governmental organizations) want in reports. Once this has been determined, work can be undertaken to improve their qualitative and quantitative aspects (see figure I). The results of this work could lead to the development of general and sectoral guidelines for environmental reporting and of performance indicators. Ultimately, such guidelines would facilitate the process of benchmarking - that is, the comparison of the environmental performance of companies with that of the leaders in the sector.

In the area of environmental auditing, it was felt that UNCTAD should take no action at the present time. It was noted that one of the constraints on opening up the conventional accounting model to environmental considerations was the reluctance of some auditors to attest to environmental information. This was understandable given the poor quality of some of the data. However, when environmental data are presented in the annual report or a separate report, users must have the expectation that they are reliable.

Besides activities in the above areas, the creation of an electronic bulletin board was discussed. Although many networks and bibliographies exist, they are incomplete. The link between researchers and experts in North America and Europe is weak. Furthermore, there is a need to make information and training available to developing countries and countries in transition so they can participate in and benefit from recent developments. It was suggested that as a first step UNCTAD update its bibliography on environmental accounting, which it published in 1992. However, it should be selective, as most people felt that one could quickly become overwhelmed by the amount of material on the environment. UNCTAD should work towards establishing an electronic bulletin board and should start with a home page on the Internet.

The group discussed the necessity for training and education in environmental accounting both in developed and developing countries. Awareness must be raised in these countries of the developments in the field. It is especially important in developing countries to train the accounting profession, standard-setters and regulators so that they can implement any guidance offered by ISAR. Since UNCTAD has an advisory service and since it has extensive experience in conducting intensive training, it would not be hard to disseminate the above outputs by means of workshops and short courses. UNCTAD should work together in the development of educational curricula and training materials with those already active in environmental accounting education. The participant from Bangladesh expressed particular interest in UNCTAD's undertaking an environmental accounting workshop in his country. In this regard a project proposal and outline have been prepared; unfortunately, however, donor funds have so far not been identified.

It was hoped that the above activities would also make a contribution to the development of accounting for sustainable development. It was felt that it was difficult to tackle the topic directly. However, by exploring developments in management accounting and by expanding the conventional financial accounting model some progress might be made.

Notes

[1]   This chapter was prepared with the assistance of Roger Adams, Chartered Association of Certified Accountants, United Kingdom.

[2]   Pp. 108-111.

[3]   "Management and reporting of environmental liabilities", *Management Accounting*, August 1995,   pp. 48-54.

[4]   Environmental Protection Agency, *An Introduction to Environmental Accounting as a Business Management Tool*, Washington, D.C., 1995, pp. 38-39.

[5]   It is reported in KPMG's *Survey of Environmental Reporting* (1994) that 66 per cent of the United Kingdom's top 100 companies and 35 per cent of all listed companies provide some form of environmental disclosure.

[6]   *Conclusions on Accounting and Reporting by Transnational Corporations*, (UNCTAD/ DTCI/1), pp. 31-32.

Bibliography

Australia

Australian Accounting Standards Board (AASB)

* AAS 7/AASB 1022, Accounting for the Extractive Industries
* Urgent Issues Group (Abstract 4), Disclosure of Accounting Policies and Restoration Obligations

Australian Society of Certified Public Accountants

* Environmental Issues: A Challenge for Management Accountants (1994)

Canada

Canadian Institute of Chartered Accountants (CICA)

* Section 3060 CICA Handbook, Future Removal and Site Restoration Costs
* Environmental Costs and Liabilities: Accounting and Financial Reporting Issues (1993)
* Environmental Reporting in Canada: a Survey of 1993 Reports (1994)
* Reporting on Environmental Performance (1994)

Society of Management Accountants of Canada

* Accounting for the Environment (1992)

Denmark

Price Waterhouse

* The Annual Environmental Report: Measuring and Reporting Environmental Performance (1995)

Europe

The European Commission's Accounting Advisory Forum (ECAAF)

* Environmental Issues in Financial Reporting (draft only)

European Federation of Financial Analysts' Societies

* Environmental Reporting and Disclosures: The Financial Analyst's View

Germany

Federal Environment Agency

* Corporate Environmental Reports (Peglau, 1995)

Institut für ökologische Wirtschaftsforschung (IOW)

* Modellprojekt Umweltkostenmanagement: Abschlussbericht (the Kunert AG flow cost accounting project) (1995)

International

Business Council for Sustainable development

*   Internalizing Environmental Costs to Promote Eco-Efficiency (1994)

World Industry Council for the Environment (WICE)

*   Environmental Reporting: A Manager's Guide (1994)

World Wildlife Fund

*   Real Value for Nature (1995)

Italy

Fondazione Eni Enrico Mattei (FEEM)

*   A Practical Approach to Integrated Environmental Accounting: the Agip Petroli Case Study (1995)

Switzerland

Swiss Association for Financial Analysis and Investment Management

*   Information Policy of Swiss Public Companies in 1994 (1995)

United Kingdom

Business in the Environment

*   City Analysts and the Environment (1994)

Chartered Association of Certified Accountants (OKAY)

*   The Greening of Accountancy (Gray, 1990)
*   Accounting for the Environment (Gray, Bebbington and Walters, 1993)
*   Environmental, Ethical and Employee Reporting in Europe (Adams, Hill and Roberts, 1995)

Chemical Industries Association (CIA)

*   The United Kingdom Indicators of Performance 1994 (1995)

Confederation of British Industry (CBI)

*   Introducing Environmental Reporting: Guidelines for Business (1994)

Institute of Chartered Accountants in England and Wales (ICAEW)

*   Financial Reporting of Environmental Liabilities: A Discussion Paper

United Nations

*   Information Disclosure Relating to Environmental Measures (E/C.10/AC.3/1990/5)
*   Accounting for Environmental Protection Measures (E/C.10/AC.3/1991/5)

* Environmental Disclosures: International Survey of Corporate Reporting Practices E/C.10/AC.3/1992/3 and E/C.10/AC.3/1994/4)
* Environmental Accounting: Current Issues, Abstracts and Bibliography (ST/CTC/SER.B/9)
* Incentives and Disincentives for the Adoption of Sustainable Development by Transnational Corporations (TD/B/ITNC/AC.1/3)
* Disclosure by Transnational Corporations of Environmental Matters at the National Level in Annual Reports (TD/B/ITNC/AC.1/4)
* Review of National Environmental Accounting Laws and Regulations (TD/B/ITNC/AC.1/2)
* The Integration of Environmental Performance Indicators with Financial Information by Transnational Corporations (TD/B/ITNC/AC.1/5)
* Accounting for Sustainable Forestry Management: A Case Study (UNCTAD/DTCI/4)

United States of America

American Institute of Certified Public Accountants (AICPA)

* (Draft) Statement of Position on Environmental Remediation Liabilities (1995)

Environmental Protection Agency (EPA)

* An Introduction to Environmental Accounting as a Business Management Tool (1995)
* Design for the Environment: Directory of EPA's Environmental Network for Managerial Accounting and Capital Budgeting (1995)

Financial Accounting Standards Board (FASB)

* FAS 5, Accounting for Contingencies
* FIN 14, Reasonable Estimation of the Amount of a Loss
* EITF 89 - 13, Accounting for the Costs of Asbestos Removal
* EITF 90 - 8, Capitalization of Costs to Treat Environmental Contamination

Harvard Business School

* Polaroid: Managing Environmental Responsibilities and Their Costs (Epstein, 1994)

Institute of Management Accountants

* Management and Reporting of Environmental Liabilities: The Chevron Case Study, *Management Accounting*, August 1995

Public Environmental Reporting Initiative

* The PERI Guidelines (1994)

Price Waterhouse

* Tackling Corporate America's Environmental Challenge (1992)
* Environmental Costs: Accounting and Disclosure (1992)
* Accounting for Environmental Compliance: Crossroads of GAAP, Engineering and Government (1992)

Securities and Exchange Commission (SEC)

* FRR 36, Interpretative Release on Management's Discussion and Analysis
* Staff Accounting Bulletin (SAB) 92, Interpretation of GAAP Regarding Contingent Liabilities
* Richard Y. Roberts: Overview of Environmental Liability Disclosure Requirements: Recent Developments and Materiality (transcript of speech, 1993)

World Resources Institute

* Green Ledgers: Case Studies in Corporate Environmental Accounting, (1995)